The Great Core Curriculum Debate is available from Change Magazine Press, P.O. Box 2023, New Rochelle, N.Y. 10802, for $7.95, postage paid.

This book was in part supported by a grant from the Carnegie Corporation

THE GREAT
CORE CURRICULUM
DEBATE

Education as a Mirror of Culture

Change Magazine Press

Acknowledgments: Chapter II is reprinted by permission of Harvard College; Barry O'Connell's and James Q. Wilson's essays appeared earlier in *Change* Magazine (September 1978 & November 1978); Chapter V is based on a recent symposium sponsored by The College Board, and published with their permission; Chapter VI is published with the permission of Yale University.

Change Magazine Press
P.O. Box 2023
New Rochelle, N.Y. 10802

Table of Contents

Contributors

GEORGE W. BONHAM is Editor-in-Chief of <u>Change</u> Magazine and Executive Director of the Council on Learning.

BARRY O'CONNELL is Associate Professor of American Studies and English at Amherst College.

JAMES Q. WILSON is Shattuck Professor of Government at Harvard and served as the Chairman of the task force on the core curriculum.

PHYLLIS KELLER is Associate Dean of the Faculty of Arts and Sciences at Harvard University.

HENRY ROSOVSKY is Dean of the Faculty of Arts and Sciences at Harvard University. He is the Walter S. Barker Professor of Economics.

ROBERT A. DAHL, a political scientist, was Chairman of the Yale study group which reviewed the University's total undergraduate experience.

Panel Participants (Chapter V)

LOUIS T. BENEZET, Professor of Human Development and Education, State University of New York at Stony Brook.

JOEL CONARROE, Executive Director, Modern Language Association of America.

JEWEL P. COBB, Dean, Douglass College, Rutgers University.

ROBERT E. MARSHAK, Distinguished Visiting Professor at Virginia Polytechnic Institute and State University; formerly President, City College of the City University of New York.

JOHN RATTÉ, Headmaster, Loomis Chaffee School.

HENRY ROSOVSKY, Dean of the Faculty of Arts and Sciences, Harvard University.

FREDERICK RUDOLPH, Mark Hopkins Professor of History, Williams College.

EDWARD G. SPARROW, Dean, St. John's College.

ILJA WACHS, Department of English, Sarah Lawrence College.

HENRY R. WINKLER, President, University of Cincinnati.

Moderator: C. A. VanderWerf, Professor of Chemistry, University of Florida.

I

TOWARD ONE HUMAN EXPERIENCE

George W. Bonham

As we ponder the inexplicable scientific phenomena of our physical universe, we must similarly approach our human universe. In the latter, we find ourselves in the midst of an unprecedented centrifugal explosion of intellectual knowledge, the end of which is nowhere in sight. But for the human spirit the very opposite may now be true: Expanded scientific knowledge has shrunk the world to a pea, and we are pressed to a centripetal imperative—that of understanding one common, universal human experience. "In a world of sudden and cataclysmic change," Father Theodore M. Hesburgh says, "simple sanity requires some constants. Navigation requires reasonably fixed points of reference. Without navigation life today becomes irrational wandering, a journey without a homecoming, a voyage with no port of call, a story without meaning or ending."[1]

Whatever we sense about our cultural experience, that tension between epistemological dispersion and humanistic divergence is surely one of our dominant animating forces. The almost endless segmentation of knowledge is a triumph of advanced civilizations, but it is not the end-all of human aspiration and the soul's imagination.

For our colleges and universities, these fundamental dilemmas of modern culture manifest themselves in particularly interesting ways. It is facile enough to allow that the universities particularly are held hostage by the graduate and professional schools, and by the often doctrinaire tyrannies of academic departments. But this is too easy an explanation and hardly resolves the deeper issues at hand. Academic institutions do not live in a vacuum. To restore some unity and coherence of knowledge—a critical goal of any academic institution worthy of that name—is at best difficult in a time when the splintering of our culture continues unabated.

Despite such an inhospitable environment, that effort must be made. Above all, we must restore to the central goals of education competencies in literacy and critical thinking. Both were once thought critical elements of a college experience, and in fact made up the cornerstones of a university education. "From the twelfth through the early twentieth century," observes Margaret Ferguson of Yale University, "the curriculum of the western university put great emphasis on the arts of argumentation—the arts Aristotle called dialectic and rhetoric and distinguished from all other branches of human knowledge on the basis of their capacity 'to draw opposite conclusions impartially.' Teachers and students, people at every level of the university's hierarchy, were continually practicing and developing argumentative skills...the university provided a forum in which critical thinking (within certain limits) was not only allowed but encouraged.... The problem we face today...is that the enabling conditions of debate are atrophying both within the university and in its relations to society.... What I propose is that the university should spend time and some of its dwindling money on devising ways to preserve genuine intellectual debate."[2]

That is perhaps a farfetched goal, but one that is important for the colleges and universities to undertake for their own good and the good of the country. In the long run, the future of the academic enterprise will not be decided in Washington and in the states, but by what the campuses do for themselves. Nothing can be as important to their survival as their internal ability to re-ask the fundamental question: How effectively do we prepare our students for a rapidly changing world?

That self-questioning of the basic purposes of education remains one of the healthiest aspects of American higher education. It is not necessarily the best test of such exercises of redesigning the undergraduate curriculum whether such recommendations finally succeed or fail in a faculty committee. Both the 1945 Harvard General Education (Redbook) report and Daniel Bell's Columbia report on general education contributed their share to the wider general debate on these topics. Yet they had widely varied histories on their own home campuses.

This book concerns itself primarily with the 1978 Harvard Report on the Core Curriculum. While this document was designed to improve undergraduate education at Harvard College alone and at no other institution, Harvard's delineation of these issues cannot help but exert a major influence elsewhere. Thus the Harvard report bears general significance far beyond Cambridge, not as a pattern for other institutions but as a thoughtful exercise in both its intellectual and political dimensions. If for no other reason, other institutions cannot pattern themselves after Harvard because of its unparalleled wealth and academic riches. Harvard undergraduates are offered a choice of some 2,500 courses. Few other institutions are able to muster such resources. At Harvard, declining enrollments in graduate schools are also likely to free up faculty for enriched undergraduate teaching, a luxury the cost of which few other schools can afford under present economic circumstances.

As such matters are wont to be, Harvard's curriculum report is also a work of hardheaded political compromise. For the realist, such accommodations are preferred over no action whatever. For the academic idealist, however, any exercise in compromise appears a sellout of essential principles of cultural and intellectual reaffirmation. A reading of this book gives both realist and idealist an opportunity to respond to the implications of the Harvard report. All of us will inevitably end up with different conclusions, but this is perhaps the best first step toward understanding the issues at hand and the political strategies necessary for any collegiate community to address these questions.

There are now hundreds of academic institutions that are tackling these central questions concerning the vitality of their educational offerings. Some of these exercises may be more imaginative, and even more ambitious, than Harvard's. It is fruitless to compare one with the other, since each document comes out of its own moment in time, its own traditions and history. As an example of a quite different approach from Harvard's, Chapter VI excerpts from a 1972 Yale report authored by Yale political scientist Robert A. Dahl and four of his colleagues. While it directs itself purely to the future educational needs of Yale College, it contains sufficient universal observations to make it of more than local interest. Perhaps because of its very ambitious scope, the Dahl report was never accepted by the Yale community. Even Yale faculty would now be hard put to find a copy on their own campus. But the failure of adoption in no way detracts from the significance of its theme and approach.

What constitutes a twenty-first-century "basic" education for young men and women remains a matter of vastly variable interpretation. For the academic world, there are now all sorts of functional reasons not to rock the boat. But if the colleges and universities themselves are tempted to lie low in this matter, there are surely more transcendent causes for cultural anxiety: For what they are putting out is a legion of technocrats and specialists, quite unprepared to deal and survive in a world that defines civic competence in ways unspecified and ignored in the biology or law curriculum. For the colleges and universities there will be no single road to salvation. But by their very exercise of deliberating curricular options, their sense of institutional purpose will be inevitably revitalized. And so will the undergraduate experience. If we are fortunate, it may reflect the human condition as a truer mirror of contemporary culture.

[1]*The Third Century*, Change Magazine Press, 1977, p. 190.
[2]*Yale Magazine and Journal*, November 1977, p. 11.

II

THE HARVARD CORE
CURRICULUM

*Shortly after assuming the presidency of Harvard University,
Derek Bok turned his attention to undergraduate education.
His annual report for 1971-72 noted much vitality, diversity,
and strength in the students and faculty of the college. But he
also observed that there was no general understanding at
Harvard—or indeed at other American colleges—of what
young men and women could expect to gain from a liberal
arts education.*

*Almost all liberal arts curricula since the early years of this
century have been organized according to principles of depth
and breadth which encourage students to acquire a solid
grasp of one subject and broad exposure to a variety of other
fields. At midcentury, breadth was provided by requiring
courses that surveyed the three main divisions of knowledge
(humanities, social sciences, and natural sciences) and offered
a grounding in the traditions and culture of Western civilization. But in the last decade or more, this curricular pattern
has seemed inadequate or inappropriate. Colleges now serve
an extraordinarily diverse body of students; knowledge has
proliferated and familiar lines of demarcation have broken
down; there is a growing interest in the history and problems
of non-Western countries and peoples. These currents have*

made it increasingly difficult to agree upon a body of knowledge that could be considered essential to the education of undergraduates, and they have called into question the structure of the traditional liberal arts curriculum.

In the summer of 1973, President Bok appointed a new dean of the faculty of arts and sciences, who immediately set out to clarify the educational goals of Harvard College. As the first step in initiating a broad review of the college, Dean Henry Rosovsky published a "Letter to the Faculty on Undergraduate Education" in October 1974. This letter outlined the problems of undergraduate education at Harvard, many of them the result of more than 25 years of unsystematic, piecemeal change in requirements and the curriculum. It called upon the faculty to join in the effort to redefine the aims and methods of liberal education.

The following spring, Dean Rosovsky appointed seven separate task forces to study different aspects of the college: the composition of the student body, college life, advising and counseling, pedagogical improvement, educational resources, concentrations, and the core curriculum. The Task Force on the Core Curriculum, chaired by Professor James Q. Wilson, was charged with determining what, if any, intellectual experiences and skills should be required of all students, regardless of their field of concentration, and how the college might best fulfill its obligation to provide a liberal education. This task force issued a preliminary report in the fall of 1976. Recommending a set of nonconcentration requirements keyed to specific educational goals, it examined and rejected arguments for the principal curricular alternatives: an expansion of electives; greater emphasis on preprofessional or vocational training; or continuation of vaguely defined distribution requirements. The so-called Wilson Report made the case for a mandatory core curriculum based not on some theoretical division or hierarchical ordering of knowledge, but rather on "distinctive ways of thinking that are identifiable and important." It offered a provisional statement of requirements in eight areas.

The Wilson Report was widely discussed in the spring of

1977. The Faculty Council (steering committee of the faculty) prepared legislation incorporating the basic recommendation while altering and consolidating the provisional statement of requirements. In May 1977, the faculty voted by a considerable majority to reaffirm its commitment to nonconcentration requirements and to proceed, through five faculty committees, to more detailed and specific recommendations.

These committees met during 1977-78, first separately, then as a committee of the whole under the chairmanship of Dean Rosovsky. The Report on the Core Curriculum, finally submitted to the faculty in April 1978, contained sections on the rationale of the core and its relation to the remainder of the undergraduate curriculum. Defining a standard of intellectual breadth, it emphasized basic modes of understanding that are important in the contemporary world. In accordance with the principles and guidelines outlined below, the faculty voted to establish a core curriculum requirement and a standing committee to implement it over a four-year period, beginning in the fall of 1979. This document is an edited version of the Report on the Core Curriculum; it incorporates modifications called for in the faculty legislation.

I. Purpose of the Core Curriculum

In his annual report for 1975-76, Dean Rosovsky attempted to state what it means to be an educated person in the latter part of the twentieth century. The standard that he outlined provided the context for the review of undergraduate education at Harvard, including the development of the core curriculum. The elements of this standard, which broadly outline the educational goals of the college, were as follows.

1. An educated person must be able to think and write clearly and effectively.

2. An educated person should have achieved depth in some field of knowledge. Cumulative learning is an effective way to develop a student's powers of reasoning and analysis, and for undergraduates this is the main role of concentrations.

3. An educated person should have a critical appreciation of the ways in which we gain and apply knowledge and understanding of the universe, of society, and of ourselves. Specifically, he or she should have an informed acquaintance with the aesthetic and intellectual experience of literature and the arts; with history as a mode of understanding present problems and the processes of human affairs; with the concepts and analytic techniques of modern social science; and with the mathematical and experimental methods of the physical and biological sciences.

4. An educated person is expected to have some understanding of, and experience in thinking about, moral and ethical problems. It may well be that the most significant quality in educated persons is the informed judgment which enables them to make discriminating moral choices.

5. Finally, an educated American, in the last third of this century, cannot be provincial in the sense of being ignorant of other cultures and other times. It is no longer possible to conduct our lives without reference to the wider world within which we live. A crucial difference between the educated and the uneducated is the extent to which one's life experience is viewed in wider contexts.

The first goal—that our students learn to communicate with precision, cogency, and force—is addressed by the requirement in expository writing and reinforced throughout the curriculum. The second goal—depth of knowledge in a particular field—is accomplished through the requirement that students concentrate a substantial portion of their work in a single subject. The importance and value of concentration were reaffirmed by both the Task Force on the Core Curriculum and the Task Force on Concentrations.

The third, fourth, and fifth goals are met specifically through the core curriculum. Its purpose is to assure that all students, regardless of their special fields of concentration, acquire the knowledge, skills, and habits of thought that the faculty believes to be of general and lasting intellectual significance. Broadly stated, the goal of the core is to encourage a critical appreciation of the major approaches to knowledge, so that students may acquire an understanding of what kinds of knowledge exist in certain important areas, how such knowledge is created, how it is used, and what it might mean to them personally. We seek, in other words, to have students acquire basic literacy in major forms of intellectual discourse.

To this end we have established requirements in five areas. Requirements in Literature and the Arts will acquaint students with important literary and artistic achievements and will aim to develop a critical understanding of how man gives artistic expression to his experience of the world. History requirements will focus on major aspects of the present world viewed in historical perspective and will attempt to lead students to an understanding of the complexity of human affairs in specific situations in the past. Requirements in Social Analysis and Moral Reasoning introduce central concepts and ideas in these intellectual realms and will develop students' abilities to think systematically about fundamental aspects of individual and social life in contemporary society. Science requirements will acquaint students with basic principles of the physical, biological, and behavioral sciences and with science as a way of looking at man and the world. Finally, a Foreign Cultures requirement is designed to expand the student's range of cultural experience and to provide fresh perspectives on his or her own cultural assumptions and traditions. This aim may be achieved through appropriate core courses in Literature and the Arts, History, or Social Analysis, or in special courses in Foreign Cultures. The intention here is not only to avoid an exclusive focus on Western traditions, but to expose students to the essential and distinctive features of foreign cultures, whether Western or non-Western.

These different areas of the core curriculum are linked by a common question: How do we gain and apply knowledge and understanding of the universe, of society, and of ourselves? The underlying purpose of the core is to set a minimum standard of intellectual breadth for our students. Yet the core is not meant to stand alone. Fulfilling core requirements will consume the equivalent of about one academic year, as did the previous general education requirement. Concentration requirements will continue to involve the equivalent of about two years of academic work. Students will retain the equivalent of one academic year for electives, within which they can express their own priorities by initiating or advancing selected aspects of their intellectual development. Conjoined with these electives and work in the field of concentration, the core will provide a solid and shared base of general and liberal education for all of our students.

It is also important to note what is *not* intended in the core curriculum. We have not established an identical set of courses for all students, or an even-handed introduction to all fields of knowledge. The proliferation of knowledge and the diversity of our students make both of these goals impractical. We do not think there is a single set of Great Books that every educated person must master, and we do not think an inevitably thin survey of the traditional subject areas—humanities, social sciences, and natural sciences—is any longer useful. Nor do we think a loose distribution requirement among departmental courses can accomplish the educational priorities that we have identified. Finally, the core curriculum is not intended as a model for higher education in general. We do not believe all colleges should perform the same function or offer the same curriculum; indeed, we are dismayed by the uniformity that has come to characterize much of higher education. Our purpose is to provide the best possible education for our own students. If we are successful, others may benefit as well, but this is secondary.

II. The Core Requirement

The Core Program establishes requirements in five areas. Detailed guidelines for the courses in each area are as follows.

Area 1: Literature and the Arts

Characteristics of the courses: The common aim of these

courses is to foster a critical understanding of how man gives artistic expression to his experience of the world. Through the examination of selected major works, students will be expected to develop and refine skills of reading, seeing, and hearing; to apprehend the possibilities and limitations of the artist's chosen medium and the means available for expression; to understand the complex interplay among individual talent, artistic tradition, and historical context. In the requirement for this area the written word takes precedence over other forms of artistic expression to the extent that the study of literature is required of all students, while a choice is offered between music and fine arts.

The requirement: One half-course in literature (A), one half-course in fine arts or music (B), and one half-course dealing with humanistic culture in its broader context (C). Certain courses in Area 1 will also be designated as meeting the requirement in Area 5 (Foreign Cultures).

A. Literature: Students will choose one half-course from a specified group of courses created or adapted for the core curriculum. Each course will examine major texts in a specific genre. This organizing principle has been chosen in the belief that formal coherence will provide added depth and dimension. The courses will aim to convey an understanding of particular modes of apprehending and articulating experience; they are not intended to be solely studies in the history of a genre. What lies behind the vision of comedy or the vision of tragedy? What are the aspirations that inform the world of the epic or the world of romance? What are the inherent attitudes in the pastoral that have attracted authors to it at certain moments in history? How is poetry capable of conveying aspects of experience which prose is not? These are the kinds of questions to be addressed. We assume that in dealing with such questions students will be exposed to a variety of critical approaches, but the primary purpose of core literature courses is to show how great authors have contrived distinctive statements about timeless and universal aspects of human experience.

B. Fine Arts or Music: Students will choose one half-course, either in fine arts or in music, from a specified group of courses. All courses will incorporate instruction in the elements of visual or aural "literacy"; it is expected that this can be done through direct exposure to the works of major artists.

(1) **Fine Arts:** Courses will focus on major works of art, artists, and sites, and emphasize questions of visual form and expression. Such courses will seek to develop the capacity to make discriminating judgments and to promote understanding of the relationship between art and the culture in which it is produced. Courses may explore one or more of the media of art and ordinarily will involve a comparison of the differing approaches and products of artists in different times and places.

(2) **Music:** Each course will attempt to convey a critical understanding of musical works of art by exploring a topically defined range of music. Courses will seek to develop in students a sensitivity to the elements of musical sound and their formal integration. In order to discern the means by which major composers achieved their masterpieces, students should acquire some familiarity with the rudiments of musical language such as rhythm, melody, and harmony; with basic principles of compositional technique and fundamental concepts of musical form; with the properties of various vocal and instrumental performance media; with the development of musical styles; and with the relevance of social and historical contexts. Courses will emphasize some aspects of analysis more than others, but above all else, students are to acquire an informed awareness of musical styles, structure, and ideas.

C. **Contexts of Culture:** In addition to half-courses in fields A and B, students will choose one half-course from a specified group of contexts courses. The aim of these courses is to illustrate, where appropriate, the connection among the arts, and to place artistic achievements in their social contexts.

These courses may be organized in many ways, though they will not be traditional surveys. The following examples of subjects and approaches are intended to be suggestive, not prescriptive. (1) Some courses may focus on a specific time and place (such as Periclean Athens or Medicean Florence) and examine significant literary, artistic, and philosophical works with reference to their social and economic contexts. (2) Some courses may study aspects of a specific stylistic movement (such as Neoclassicism, Romanticism, or Impressionism) by examining in detail selected works of art and literature viewed in their social contexts. (3) Other courses may focus on a specific theme in intellectual history as it touches several cultures or nations (for example, country versus city, ideals of education, concepts of the happy man, or utopias). (4) Still other courses might look at various movements, such as renaissances or revivals, in different countries and times, considering their causes, their shared characteristics, and their effects, while linking them with social and political needs. (5) Another type of course might be concerned with certain fundamental aspects of the creative process. For example, a course might consider how certain great artists, such as Euripides, Shakespeare, Goethe, Titian, and Beethoven, achieved in their final visions a resolution of those artistic and philosophical problems with which they had wrestled through a lifetime of creativity.

All such courses will necessarily be selective in their use of artistic and literary materials, and they need not be confined to the Western tradition, though this tradition should predominate in the listings of any given year.

Area 2: Historical Study

Characteristics of the courses: These courses seek to accomplish two aims: to orient students historically to some of the major concerns of the contemporary world; and to help them acquire a measure of understanding regarding the complexity of human affairs in specific situations in the past and the process by which important changes have taken place.

The requirement: One half-course in A and one half-course in B. The requirements may be fulfilled by students at any point in their four years; indeed, freshman year may not be the best time to take a course in either field. Certain courses in both A and B will be designated as also meeting the requirement in Area 5 (Foreign Cultures).

A. Historical Orientation to the Present: The purpose of these courses is to explain historically some major aspect of the present world. Courses will be broad in scope, addressing the modern world in a global or near-global subject area. For this purpose, the "modern" world is defined as the late nineteenth and twentieth centuries; but courses that deal with extended periods of history will be included in this category if they also meet the purpose of accounting historically for important issues in the present world. Examples of areas particularly appropriate to this category are: the development of modern political ideologies; the history of international conflicts in the modern world; and main trends in politics and social organization, in modern economic history, and in modern intellectual history.

B. The Process of History: The purpose of these courses is to examine in detail the complexity of transforming events, the interactions of social and economic circumstance, belief, purpose, effort, and accident that shape people's lives. These courses will involve students in affairs that once divided people sharply but no longer do and that now may be approached impartially. Courses will deal with (1) developments that shaped some significant portion of history irreversibly; (2) issues that were controversial in their own time and that people struggled over—hence, manifest rather than latent issues; (3) issues that are not directly related to modern policy questions. These courses will include a broad view of some major transition in human affairs—origins, consolidation, and consequences—and provide sufficient detail to allow realistic judgments on particular participants, motives, perceptions, and decisions. Thus a course on the triumph of the Christian church in late classical antiquity would be appropriate here; so too would courses on the challenge of the Protestant Reformation, the struggles that ensued, and the process by which accommodations were reached; on the origins and consequences of the Thirty Years' War; on the French, American, or Russian Revolution; on the English

Civil War; and on the challenge of and struggles over Darwinism.

Area 3: Social Analysis and Moral Reasoning

Characteristics of the courses: The common aim of these courses is to introduce students to the central concepts and ideas of social science and moral and political philosophy, and to develop their analytic skills in understanding the fundamental social institutions and concerns of contemporary society. Courses will be organized around certain topics or themes chosen for their effectiveness in demonstrating how social scientists and philosophers think about social and moral issues. Courses will focus primarily, but not exclusively, on one of the following: (1) the application of a formal body of theory and of empirical data to an understanding of some fundamental aspect of individual or social life in contemporary society; or (2) the investigation of significant and recurrent questions of choice and value which arise in ordinary political and moral experience, drawing on writings of political and social theorists. Courses may include an historical or comparative dimension. They need not attempt comprehensive coverage of the work currently being done in any single discipline.

The requirement: Two half-courses, one in Social Analysis (A) and one in Moral Reasoning (B). Certain courses in Social Analysis may also be designated as meeting the requirement in Area 5 (Foreign Cultures).

A. Social Analysis: The object of these courses is to familiarize students with some of the central approaches of the social sciences and to do so in a way that gives students a sense of how those approaches can enhance their understanding of human behavior in the context of contemporary society. The courses offered to meet this part of the core requirement will provide coherent formal theories or analytical approaches that are tested or illuminated by empirical data. A core course in economics, for example, would explain the nature, assumptions, and consequences of rational choice in the context of scarce resources. A core course in anthropology might explain the meaning of culture and how it affects ways of perceiving, valuing, and acting in a social context. A core course in psychology might take as its central concept personality, motivation, or intelligence, whereas one in sociology might focus on the nature, causes, and implications of social stratification. A core course in government might explore the nature of power in governmental decision making.

In addition to exposing students to the core approaches or theories of various disciplines, courses will also expose students to the empirical data (statistical or other) used by disciplines in testing or elucidating key theories or propositions. Consideration will be given to the limitations as well as to the uses of social science data. Wherever possible, courses will explore the implicit values and assumptions underlying the analysis.

The key criteria for acceptance into the core for all courses will be whether such courses give students a systematic introduction to some major social science field and to its theoretical and empirical foundations. Introductory courses that place primary emphasis on current policy issues without explicit and substantial use of formal theories or approaches will not be eligible for inclusion.

B. Moral Reasoning: These courses will serve a multiple purpose: to introduce students to important traditions of thought, to make them aware of the intricacies of ethical argument, and to bring them to grips with particular questions of choice and value. They are to learn that it is possible to think systematically about such issues as justice, obligation, personal responsibility, citizenship, and friendship. The emphasis in this part of the core will be on Western traditions of thought and their relationship to political institutions and moral practice.

Courses will focus on ethics, law, and politics. Three different approaches to these subjects ought to be reflected in each year's core listings. First, the historical approach, involving the study of major texts organized around one, or a very few, central themes, or examining in detail moral values and beliefs at some critical period of Western history; examples might be Greek Ethics, or Citizenship in Historical Perspective. Second, a disciplinary approach stressing those concepts and issues that underlie the study of moral, political, and legal choice: determinism and responsibility, utilitarianism, the theory of rights, law and morals, legitimacy, and so on. Third, an approach in terms of concrete problems such as distributive justice, obligations, civil rights, or medical ethics, emphasizing particular moral and political controversies, legal cases, and historical examples.

Area 4: Science

Characteristics of the courses: The common aim of these courses is to help students increase their scientific literacy and their capacity to approach scientific material intelligently. A further purpose is to convey a general understanding of science as a way of looking at man and the world.

The wealth of important and fundamental scientific knowledge is immense and rapidly growing. So is the need to understand increasingly complex interrelations between science and human affairs. The core science requirement is intended to insure that every student acquires some appreciation of this vast and fundamental intellectual activity. In addition to the two half-courses required, there is a mathematics prerequisite (discussed in section IV) which will permit the core courses to assume some mathematical preparation on the part of all students.

Observations of the physical and biological world have led scientists to formulate principles that provide universal explanations of diverse phenomena. These include the laws that govern classical dynamics, thermodynamics, radiation, and the microscopic structure of matter, and the basic principles that underlie chemistry, molecular and cellular biology, biological evolution, and behavior. The core will contain courses that treat such basic scientific concepts and findings in some depth.

Every undergraduate should learn how scientists go about

understanding the world through examples that illustrate these fundamental concepts and principles. The courses should consider not only what scientists believe is true in some domain, but how they have developed and validated their laws and principles. The critical role of observation and experiment in this process should be exhibited.

Core courses need not be limited to, nor provide broad and full coverage of, a single discipline. It is hoped that a number of the courses created or adapted for the core will be inter-disciplinary in nature. Some may bring historical or social perspectives to bear, describing, for example, how commonly held views have been overturned by certain major scientific discoveries, and some of the methods and motivations of the discoverers. Several core courses should have no prerequisite other than some knowledge of mathematics (see section IV). The skills necessary to attack selected problems should be developed along the way. A number of courses, particularly in the physical sciences, may have a considerable mathematical component.

Many entering students already have a good background in the sciences. To serve these students, as well as those who wish to pursue their scientific education beyond the minimum requirement, some courses that presuppose an understanding of certain basic concepts and theories should also be offered. These courses might focus on the major principles and findings in areas of contemporary scientific research.

The requirement: Core science courses are divided into two groups. Courses in group A will deal primarily with the predictive and deductive analysis of natural phenomena through quantitative treatment of their components. Group B will contain courses that analyze more complex systems that cannot be fully reduced to the behavior of their components, and courses that provide a more descriptive, historical, or evolutionary treatment of aspects of the natural world. Students must take one half-course from each group. Approved departmental science courses at a more advanced level may also satisfy the core science requirement. Because the science requirement is intended to serve as an irreducible minimum, students are encouraged to explore this area more deeply and extensively through electives.

Area 5: Foreign Cultures

Characteristics of the courses: The common aim of all the courses is to expand the student's range of cultural experience and to provide fresh perspectives on the student's own cultural assumptions and traditions. Courses may well emphasize language as a means of entry into another culture, but proficiency should not be considered enough in itself for this purpose.

Courses need not attempt comprehensive coverage, but rather will penetrate deeply into selected aspects of the culture being studied. They may be problem-oriented, and should include consideration of the historical background and contemporary aspects of the culture under study. As much as possible, they will devote attention to religious and ethical values, social systems, intellectual trends, and literary and artistic achievements. Whether the primary emphasis is on the analysis of key texts and works of art, on historical orientation and perspective, or on fundamental aspects of individual or social life, these courses will seek to identify the distinctive patterns of thought, belief, and action that account for the particular configuration or ethos of another culture.

The foreign cultures studied in core courses will, primarily but not exclusively, be living cultures and represent major cultural traditions. For these purposes, foreign cultures may be divided into two groups, with the principle that the less "foreign" a culture, the more advanced should be its study. The Area subcommittee will determine the boundaries between the two groups on a case-by-case basis.

The requirement: For Area 5, the core requirement in Foreign Cultures may be met in any one of four ways:

A. One half-course devoted to the study of an important aspect of a major culture of the West and using the language of that culture. Courses available through this option will be listed under core Areas 1, 2, or 3 and designated as also meeting the requirement in Area 5. The core subcommittee in Foreign Cultures will develop guidelines for establishing the level of expected language proficiency. Students choosing courses through this option will be expected to deal with texts or lectures in a foreign language, but we are not disposed to tie the necessary level of proficiency to a numerical score on an existing test.

B. One half-course devoted to the study of other major cultures where, in view of the difficulty of the languages, texts would be read in translation. Courses under this option will be listed under core Areas 1, 2, or 3 and designated as also meeting the requirement in Area 5.

C. One half-course which meets the objectives of Area 5 without meeting the criteria of Areas 1, 2, or 3 (such courses might treat two or more cultures or combine a number of disciplinary approaches). If Western European cultures provide the focus of study, courses will incorporate work in the appropriate foreign languages. Students who prefer this option will, in effect, be choosing to take one half-course more than the seven or eight half-course minimum needed to meet the core requirements in all areas. It is our intention that most of the courses available through the preceding options will meet the conditions of A and B. These will be proposed, developed, and reviewed by the Foreign Cultures subcommittee, but they will be assigned to Literature and the Arts, Historical Studies, or Social Analysis by the Standing Committee on the Core Program in consultation with the subcommittees governing those Areas.

D. Selected full second-year language courses which are qualified by virtue of the subject matter treated or the cultural access provided through purely linguistic study may also meet the core requirement in Foreign Cultures. Students who prefer this option will, in effect, be choosing two half-courses in addition to the seven or eight half-course minimum needed to meet core requirements in all areas.

III. Exemptions and Modifications

The core program establishes 10 course requirements.

However, the faculty intended that the core requirement should normally require no more than the equivalent of one year of work, or eight half-courses. This temporal constraint is satisfied without jeopardizing the goals of the core as follows.

First, students will receive exemptions from one or two core fields that overlap their concentration (as determined by the standing committee) where the total concentration program satisfies the objectives of the core. Thus history concentrators would be exempted from the core requirements in Area 2, Historical Study. This will reduce core course requirements by one or two half-courses. Second, most of the courses meeting the Foreign Cultures requirement (Area 5) will also satisfy requirements in Areas 1, Literature and the Arts; 2, Historical Study; or 3, Social Analysis. This will reduce the core requirement by one half-course. Together, these two modifications diminish the requirements of the core program to seven or eight half-courses. Some core courses will count only toward the Foreign Cultures requirement; when students elect these courses, they will have to be taken in addition to the seven or eight half-courses otherwise required. Further adjustments will accommodate the special needs of transfer and advanced standing students.

Modifications which allow alternative methods of satisfying core objectives, but do not reduce the quantity of course work required for the core, were authorized in the enabling legislation. First, the standing committee and its subcommittees were encouraged to permit a specified advanced half-course in a department to count for a core requirement whose objectives it fulfills. Second, the committee was authorized and urged to designate particular "core-related sequences" containing two or more related or complementary half-courses and to allow such sequences to count for the core requirement in the field whose objectives it fulfills. Third, the committee was asked to examine alternatives which permit students to shift no more than one half-course between areas of the core. Fourth, the committee was authorized to adjust the requirements, as they relate to field specifications, on the basis of experience. All modifications made by the standing committee are to be reviewed by the full faculty in 1982-83.

IV. Other Nonconcentration Requirements

In formulating the core curriculum, the faculty also addressed certain other nonconcentration requirements in the college. Questions regarding the character of the concentration programs themselves were considered by a separate task force.

Writing: The faculty reaffirmed the importance of a requirement in expository writing and placed responsibility for that requirement in the hands of a special subcommittee within the Core Program. It also made two recommendations for improving instruction in writing at Harvard. First, expository writing instruction should be linked with courses in the core curriculum as a means of strengthening both. Second, evaluation of writing skills should be provided during the freshman orientation period; the small fraction of the class with substantial writing deficiencies will then be required to attend a noncredit remedial course during the fall term, before enrolling in a regular expository writing section in the spring term. The subcommittee is currently studying the implementation of these and other improvements in expository writing.

Foreign language: In adopting the core curriculum, the faculty affirmed the value of knowledge of a foreign language, but referred detailed study of the foreign language requirement to a special committee. Pending the outcome of this consideration, the present foreign language requirement (one year of study in college, or a score of 560 or better on a foreign language examination) remains in force.

Mathematics: Finally, the faculty voted to institute a new degree requirement asking for demonstrated competence in the application of mathematics and quantitative reasoning. Details of this requirement are currently being developed by the core subcommittee on mathematics. The emphasis will be on applications because, by and large, this is the weakest aspect of prior training in mathematics and the one most widely called upon in college studies. The vast majority of

Harvard students have taken at least 11 years of earlier math courses. In recent years the mean score of our freshmen on the SAT math test has been over 700, and almost all of our students have scores above the national average for high school seniors. But too many students are unable to use what they know in new contexts: For example, many students with a full year of college calculus had difficulty performing a simple linear extrapolation of data points in a second-year biology course.

Thus, the main thrust of the mathematics requirement will be to bridge the gap between th   student's theoretical knowledge and its application. One component will be the concept of function and its role in understanding reality. A second component will be dealing with uncertainty through the techniques of probability and statistics. In addition, students will acquire an elementary knowledge of computer programming and familiarity with the Harvard time-sharing system, providing a base for the development and application of computer skills throughout the curriculum. A large majority of students will be able to satisfy the mathematics requirement by test, without having to enroll in a formally organized course. Self-study guides will be available, along with informal lectures and individual help provided at a question center; tests will be offered at frequent intervals. But for students who choose or need a more extensive and structured treatment, we will also offer a regular course covering the material of the mathematics requirement.

V. Implementation

Since the careful development or adaptation of courses suited to the purposes of the Core Program will take considerable time, the core requirements will be gradually implemented over a four-year period. The freshmen of fall 1979, the class of '83, are subject to the earlier general education requirement, but their general education program must include core courses from at least two fields. The class of '84 must take core courses in at least four fields. The class of '85 must take core courses in at least six fields. The full core requirements will apply to students in the class of '86 and beyond. The mathematics requirement will first apply to the class of '84, entering in the fall of 1980. During the transition, the general education portion of the requirement may be satisfied by current general education courses, by core courses, or by the existing departmental bypass (two departmental courses equal one general education course).

Core courses, first offered in 1979-80, will increase in number in following years. Once implementation is complete, the overall core curriculum should offer between 80 and 100 courses each year. Thus, on average, eight to ten courses will be available in each field in any given year.

The standing committee will report to the faculty annually on the status of the Core Program. The full Core Program and its requirements will be subject to review and approval by the full faculty in the academic year 1982-83.

Principal contributors to the Report on the Core Curriculum were: Bernard Bailyn, Derek C. Bok, Glen W. Bowersock, Harvey Brooks, John L. Clive, John E. Dowling, Donald L. Fanger, Stanley H. Hoffmann, Walter J. Kaiser, Edward L. Keenan, Phyllis Keller, Paul C. Martin, Dwight H. Perkins, Edwin O. Reischauer, Henry Rosovsky, Michael L. Walzer, Charles P. Whitlock, Edward T. Wilcox, James Q. Wilson.

III

WHERE DOES HARVARD
LEAD US?

Barry O'Connell

The only use of knowledge of the past is to equip us for the present. No more deadly harm can be done to young minds than by depreciation of the present. The present contains all that there is. It is holy ground; for it is the past and it is the future.

Alfred North Whitehead, *The Aims of Education*

Recent efforts of colleges to reform their curricula claim our attention. Amid the often trivial details of course requirements, faculty debates, and reports, we have ample reason to search for those significant changes which promise to help us meet the present that Whitehead describes. Our present, late in the twentieth century, threatens to overwhelm us. Few people, upon reflection, see a benign future for our society or for the world. Many have lost the will to work for a better future; the rest feel baffled by the complexities of our problems. Genuine democracy daily declines as a force in our political life; the economy of advanced capitalism becomes less and less rational; and at the darkest moments a selfish individualism destructive of every common good possesses us. We must confront the present, yet we know not how. We depend upon political and educational institutions for leadership, yet these institutions are themselves in disarray.

Each citizen rightly has his own notions of the most pressing needs in our society. But many lack the means of articulating their ideas, the power to act upon them, and the credentials our culture uses to confer on some the right to be heard and the opportunity to lead. American universities, especially the most prestigious, help maintain this inequality, which is perhaps the major barrier to a movement toward a decent future. They, almost exclusively, bestow the aura of qualification which creates a presumptive claim to privilege and leadership. Daniel Bell puts it succinctly: "Today, with

---

The curriculum recently adopted in Cambridge is neither original nor particularly distinguished. The Harvard "core" is, at best, a watered-down version of the experiments in general education conducted at Columbia in the 1920s, at Hutchins's Chicago in the 1930s, and at Harvard itself in the late 1940s.

---

higher education as the chief route of social mobility, the elite universities *determine* the new status positions of the post-industrial society. The singular fact is that a small number of universities have become the channels to place and position in the society." Harvard places first among the 14 elite universities Bell names.

In view of this finding, it would seem reasonable to expect that reforms undertaken within a university would address the connection between higher education and social mobility within the society at large. I have examined proposals for restructuring the curriculum at 25 institutions. Few of them, and Harvard is no exception, confront this issue. Most simply urge some restoration of the degree requirements modified in the sixties. Many, Harvard prominently among them, recommend some version of a core curriculum. Institutions as different as Amherst, Brigham Young University, Emory, the University of Richmond, Middlebury, Saint Joseph's College in Indiana, and the University of Pennsylvania are considering, or have already adopted, new general education programs. The specific details differ, but the pattern is essentially similar. Each hopes to broaden students' learning and to engage faculty in more extradepartmental teaching.

These schools propose that each student generalize his or her education by taking courses in Western and non-Western civilizations, social and political analysis, ethics, science and mathematics, and in the humanities and the arts. Some through courses, others through competency examinations also expect each student to achieve facility in another language, in expository writing, and in quantitative reasoning. A few colleges, while not following this pattern, are attempting to achieve the same ends by reimposing distribution requirements (as at Berkeley or Hamline University in St. Paul). Others, like Stanford, might in a limited way follow the Chicago and Columbia general education programs by recommending a single course in Western civilization for all students. At Stanford, though, this effort has been undermined by the faculty's reluctance to offer a common course taught in small sections, since it would require them to teach beyond their specialties.

Most proposals genuflect dutifully to the usual clichés about the knowledge explosion, the expansion of the universities, and the problem of specialization. Little institutional self-examination occurs, and when it does it covers a narrow range: what new courses are needed, what means can be devised to improve teaching, how best to cope with financial stringencies. Only a few documents inquire about the reasons for poor teaching, the fragmentation of the faculty, or the existence of thoughtlessly designed departmental majors. The few such inquiries I read tend to grandiose rhetoric (such as those of the University of Pennsylvania and the University of Wisconsin-Stout). Most of the proposed reforms are, with a disheartening frequency, mechanical and bureaucratic. More committees are recommended; vague guidelines are promulgated for faculty to meet in whatever individual fashion they choose. The crucial questions—about the role of the university in maintaining inequality and about the desired ends of an undergraduate education—are left untouched.

The curriculum recently adopted in Cambridge is neither original nor particularly distinguished. The Harvard "core" is, at best, a watered-down version of the experiments in general education conducted at Columbia in the 1920s, at Hutchins's Chicago in the 1930s, and at Harvard itself in the late 1940s. Compared with the report of the 1945 committee at Harvard, *General Education in a Free Society*, it falls disappointingly short of expectations. The writers of the so-called *Redbook* sought to examine the whole of the American educational system and only within that context to address Harvard's special needs and possibilities. They wished to define an education appropriate to people's roles as citizens in a democracy as part of their argument for the necessity of creating a common democratic culture. Their successors at Harvard are notable in contrast only for the narrowness of their reflections.

The Harvard curriculum, unoriginal though it is, can instruct us about the nature of the crisis we actually face. Inertia in the large and more prestigious institutions plays a major part. Anyone who teaches in higher education knows how difficult it is to persuade a majority of one's colleagues to change a curriculum, reform a departmental major, or to reflect productively on the shape of the extracurriculum. Because faculties resist change, we perhaps should be uncritical when an institution like Harvard concludes a lengthy curricular review with some fresh resolution. Harvard, so far in this decade, stands out among universities of its rank and size in having actually adopted any substantial reform. Yale's faculty in 1973 rejected the Dahl committee's far more original, ingenious, and promising proposals. Princeton earlier failed to act. Berkeley and Stanford have made minor alterations in their curricula while claiming more significant changes. Chicago and Columbia, with some revisions, have maintained their commitments to a strong general education program.

At Harvard, only the steady commitment of the president and a dean of the faculty chosen for his interest in reform, his political adroitness, and his toughness made any change possible. Even with the work of these two crucial officers, the outcome was in considerable doubt. Dean Henry Rosovsky began the process in 1974 with a letter to his colleagues. He followed it with the creation of task forces on the Core Curriculum, Composition of the Student Body, Pedagogical Improvement, Concentrations, Advising and Counseling, Educational Resources, and Student Life. The preliminary report of the crucial committee on the core curriculum led to the appointment of five more committees, each charged with examining areas proposed for inclusion in the core. These committees were, in turn, transformed into a single committee out of which the final recommendations to the faculty emerged. The particular curricular proposals are less significant than the committee's recommendation that eight new committees be charged with implementing the new curriculum, which remains only the vaguest of paper designs. One committee will oversee the rest while the other seven supervise the curricular areas in the proposed core.

A new curriculum does not yet exist. Four years and countless hours of committee work brought a faculty vote agreeing to the outline of the requirements for a core. "Core" is, in truth, a misnomer since the faculty in the next several years will create or redesignate no fewer than 80 and no more than 100 courses that students may take to fulfill the requirements. Not until 1983 will the curriculum finally be in place. Harvard will then have spent nearly 10 years in the creation of the program—an expensive process in faculty energy and time, and in money, which few institutions could afford to take as a model.

A dispassionate observer might conclude that Harvard has shaped the ideal curriculum for a corporate future. Its mode of design and its form of operation provide a model of bureaucracy. Like all effective bureaucracies, this one seems likely to specialize in persuading its clients that everything it does is in their best interests, while using the appearance of responsiveness to dilute dissent and to hinder clear thinking about the ends of the institution. This may be reform, but at least on paper it looks more like administrative reorganization. If changes in higher education are imperative, the kind of bureaucracy required at universities like Harvard seems certain to defeat anything of value. Inertia necessitates so many compromises as to deprive Harvard, and those who might look to it, of just the sharp critical discourse we must have to respond intelligently to the needs of our colleges.

The areas recommended for the core are unsurprising. Students are to become acquainted with literature and the arts (three semester-long courses), with history (two), with social and philosophical analysis (two), science and mathematics (two), and with a foreign language or culture (one). Each student must also demonstrate a reading knowledge of a foreign language, an ability to express him- or herself in writing, and a basic mathematical competence (whether to the level of algebra or calculus is undecided). The education of the body through physical activity in athletics or in the arts goes unmentioned. Visual literacy, arguably essential in a culture dominated by the visual media, is equally unattended. These are not mere additions to a laundry list of requirements any of us might conceive. Harvard's conception of the essentials of a good education in 1978 is limited to subjects most scholars in 1900 would have regarded as the core. The anachronistic thinking evident in its new curriculum is not a matter of the inclusion of the traditional liberal arts, but of a failure to appreciate the centrality of new modes of understanding to our present lives.

Students today need, and ask for, opportunities through which they might venture to connect intellectual and practical activities—in the arts, in physical exercise, in community projects. An attempt to meet this need might help them believe they could effect some reforms in themselves and in society. More encounters with the difficulty and the art of transformation, with the movement from what one imagines to what one can make tangible, would do much to help students discover the patient discipline necessary if they are to avoid the paralysis so many say they feel. Another educational gain might also be accomplished with the inclusion of these subjects in a required curriculum: Few students (understandably, given their age) come to college with any compelling sense of what they must know. Once introduced to a subject or a mode of inquiry, they too readily believe they understand what they have yet to encounter.

The Harvard reforms reveal other failures of imagination and will. Each of them, while not easily explicable, derives from a reverence for departmental prerogatives, the great sacred cow in the academy. If, for instance, students ought to

---

If changes in higher education are imperative, the kind of bureaucracy required at universities like Harvard seems certain to defeat anything of value.

---

be acquainted with the history of a non-Western culture—as the Harvard curriculum proposes—then a one-semester course is simply insufficient. Two courses in science and mathematics are similarly inadequate. The problem might be resolved in one of two ways, but both would infringe on departmental preserves. More courses could be required outside the major; or, preferably, the departments might themselves be required to include more integrative courses in their offerings, at least at the introductory level.

Departmental power sustains the inertia afflicting Harvard and other universities. The deliberations at Harvard failed from the beginning to examine departmental majors, the primary determinant of the undergraduate curriculum. Dean

Rosovsky could compliment the Harvard faculty in 1974 for
its "persistent and intense self-scrutiny," when an outsider
can find little evidence of this capacity in the lengthy process
of curricular debate. The dean himself, in this same letter calling for a curricular review, excused the departments from
scrutiny: "Departmental concentrations are normally well
designed and taught. I might point out that this favorable
assessment has never, to my knowledge, been seriously challenged either at Harvard or elsewhere." Yet, in the same document, he earlier refers to the "blur of concentrations" and
explains the malaise of the General Education Program as a
result of "the primacy of the disciplines and the pull of the
departments."

His exoneration of the departments may have been a
necessary political gesture, but the excuse tells us much about
the obstacles to genuine reform. The subsequent report of the
Task Force on the Concentrations is even more timid. It finds
little to criticize and recommends essentially no change. Its
only substantial recommendations, significantly, are directed
at the few interdisciplinary concentrations at Harvard. These
recommendations may well undermine or even destroy these
valuable and, at Harvard, unusual enterprises.

Harvard's final curriculum committee conceded that it did
not feel "competent to design a specific program of study outside of the concentrations but had seen its mission as...estab-
lishing individual committees of experts in various areas to
recommend...the specific content of the core program." The
acknowledgment suggests the incapacity of a departmental-
ized faculty to reflect interestingly upon, or to agree about,
the ends of undergraduate education. The curriculum committee, in effect, resigned its task to the departments, the "experts" in the university. Students need a broader education
than they commonly receive, but the focus on their narrowness appears misplaced. The more compelling need is for
teachers who are both committed to general education and
trained to engage in it. The 70-year dominance of American
universities by the departments has kept us from obtaining
the kinds of teachers and scholars indispensable to the educa-

tional enterprise. The faculty itself, and not just at Harvard, may require a general education before it can offer the same to students.

Graduate education, then, may well be the linchpin of the whole system. Until it is reformed we will have few teachers or scholars prepared to teach outside their departments or sufficiently trained to perceive the ways in which disciplines now increasingly intersect. Here, too, the Harvard process failed. At the same time Dean Rosovsky absolved the departments from scrutiny, he excluded graduate education from review: "Within the sphere of educational policy, the problems posed by graduate training should be debated and resolved primarily within departments. But the problems and questions of purpose posed by undergraduate education require the broadest possible consideration." This is a bit like asking the culprits to be the sheriffs and the judges. It appears willfully naive to call for "the broadest possible consideration" of undergraduate education while implying that graduate education has nothing much to do with it. Graduate education absorbs the energies of faculty in all the major universities. This, with the faculty's own intense professionalism, has distorted many majors into preprofessional programs.

Harvard's pretensions to leadership here collapse into irresponsibility. Harvard's influence upon graduate education is great; at least in this sphere it might conceivably have exerted genuine leadership, but it did not even choose to recognize the opportunity. If faculty are unwilling or unable to be models, it borders on hypocrisy to demand of undergraduates that they eschew narrowness and become acquainted with the major questions and modes of analysis in a wide range of fields. Some kind of core curriculum in graduate programs has much to recommend it. Students would encounter other disciplines, having some competence in a single discipline. Their maturity and knowledge might also encourage them to insist that such training demonstrate its usefulness to their own particular inquiries. The academic profession reproduces itself in the graduate schools. If students learn there that a narrow preparation insufficiently trains them for the scholarly and pedagogical life, then we could anticipate an actual transformation in the undergraduate college. We might also begin to get more scholars and teachers who understand they have vital responsibilities beyond the department, even beyond the university, to the education of all members of the society. Otherwise, for the sake of honesty, we ought to forgo our titles and be called what we have virtually become—assistant, associate, or full technicians.

The problems many advocates of the new curricula, at Harvard and elsewhere, claim to alleviate, or to solve, originated long before the past decade. Students' vocational fixations are hardly new, nor are they discouraged by the very institutions whose faculties now deplore them. The knowl-

---

If faculty are unwilling or unable to be models, it borders on hypocrisy to demand of undergraduates that they eschew narrowness and become acquainted with the major questions and modes of analysis in a wide range of fields.

---

edge explosion happened long ago. Specialization was well established and amply criticized by the end of Charles Eliot's tenure at Harvard. The elective system has prevailed in American education for almost a century. General education reforms decades ago proved unable either to check the elective system or to challenge the departments. The historical record makes evident that the terms of the present debate have been central to every critical examination of the academy for at least 80 years.

Why, then, all the attention to Harvard? Are we simply being gulled by the media's—and our own—inclinations to deference? One must almost believe so, given the alacrity with which the media have fastened onto the new Harvard curriculum as the solution to all our woes. *Saturday Review* reverently calls it "a quiet revolution" which promises to end the "anarchy" rampaging on the nation's campuses. The *New York Times*, no less, announces the end of the crisis as quickly as it seems to have been discovered: "So nothing will have been lost if the Harvard way becomes the nation's way." Surely even the problems these commentators cite are too great to be resolved by the changes in a single institution.

Harvard has attracted notice for its prestige, of course, but also because its new curriculum so easily can be taken as the nostrum for what ails us. Yet much more is at issue than has been acknowledged. An examination which clearly formulated the deeper problems in higher education would raise questions neither the universities nor much of the society is prepared to face. I suspect it is for this reason that the media and many faculties have produced such superficial analyses and reforms.

In our time the universities have become the principal manufacturers and retailers of knowledge as a commodity—a transformation Clark Kerr vividly characterized in *The Uses of the University*. Universities have many buyers: students seeking credentials to insure prosperous futures, industries wanting the skills and products of faculty researchers, and the government needing an array of services. Something of substance is often exchanged in these transactions, but equally important to the purchasers are the intangibles of prestige, authority, and expertise the university confers.

Radical students in the sixties challenged the legitimacy of these academic functions. They argued that the university justified privilege and served the ends of power. The university might harbor some dissenters but this could not excuse its principal activities. Few faculty members accepted these criticisms. Many perhaps regretted what the university had become but remained silent or insisted that there was no returning to the older ideal of the university as a place apart, the source of critical insight, and even of opposition to the status quo.

Faculties across the nation made only one coherent response to these challenges. They abolished most of the degree requirements outside the major. It seems a curious response, since few radicals criticized the curriculum. But the abolition appealed because it seemed to express sympathy, though not agreement, with students and, most importantly, because it freed faculty from tasks many did not want—the teaching of courses outside their specialization and the regulation of students' extracurricular lives. It actually brought to culmination the historical process whereby the universities became purely the purveyors of credentials and technical knowledge.

The present student generation is repeating the experience of students in the sixties—with a different consequence. Students come to college now, as they did then, deeply troubled about the world they inhabit, skeptical about the capacity of most institutions to redress the apparently intransigent failures of our society, but hopeful that their educations might provide them with the understanding and the skills necessary to better the world they inherit. Their hopes are more tempered than those of their predecessors, their faith tipped toward cynicism and resignation. They nonetheless look to their teachers and to the academy itself. They want what the sixties radicals, or at least the best of them, wanted: an education, to paraphrase Whitehead, to develop their human capacity to attend experience, to teach them to think against what is, to imagine otherness, and to propose alternative ways of being, of organizing experience, societies, economies, and politics.

What do these often desperate and wary students find, especially in the elite institution, an adult culture which nearly mirrors the society at large? Teaching is, for the most part, honored mainly in public relations releases. The highest rewards go to those who pursue their special fields as intensely as possible. Faculty members appear primarily devoted to professional advancement and uninterested in a community of teachers and learners. The education of people for life in a democratic society is scarcely attempted. The proffered education is instead directed to reproducing the academic profession or to enhancing some students' competitive edge in the mobility race. Departments reign supreme, and the question of curriculum is relegated to their supervision with an occasional gesture toward a general, integrated education.

Students are quick to read the cues of their elders. Even in anticipation of college, they become obsessed with their professional futures. Once enrolled they grow fully disillusioned, more quickly than in the sixties. Resignation and privatism replace open rebellion and political engagement. They elect courses in which they will earn high grades and directly prepare for the vocations they have chosen. They compete intensely because they know the universities produce many more graduates than there are desirable jobs or places in professional schools. What idealism remains is translated into a hope for a career of decency and some human usefulness, a private life of virtue and a public life held in abeyance.

The process does not conduce to much self-respect among the current student generation. Having lost their faith, as it were, they must now endure the excoriations of their teachers and the media for being narrowly obsessed with career, and, if one believes most of the curricular reports, inept at writing, incompetent in mathematics, and moral barbarians. I do not intend to portray students as wholly innocent. It bears remembering, however, that they bring to the academy the gifts and blindness the young have always brought. They are eager for guidance, anxious to learn for the most part, aspiring idealists when not full-fledged ones. They are also scared, ignorant, and dependent on those society tells them are older and wiser. What I wish to suggest is that the war against the young that Richard Poirier found central to the sixties continues in a new guise in this decade.

Students are no worse educated than they ever were. While it is notoriously difficult to document reliably what undergraduates actually learn, in part because the universities are reluctant to test their effects on students, no existing evidence demonstrates that this generation of students is any more illiterate in English, or ignorant of history, mathematics, the sciences, and ethics than any previous generation. A decent case could be made that they are better educated. A commission appointed to investigate the recent decline in College Board scores admitted that it could not be sure of the causes. Its members strongly suspected that the decline resulted from the increased numbers of students of working-class and minority backgrounds taking the tests—those students most disadvantaged in our public schools. This conclusion suggests that those Americans who have traditionally gone to college are at least as well, or as poorly, prepared as ever.

People unquestionably need greater understanding of the subjects now proposed as essential to the core: science and mathematics, the history of Western and non-Western civilizations, modes of social and political analysis, the great works of the humanities and art, philosophical and moral reflection. The provision of these subjects, however, will not of itself begin to meet the fundamental problems in higher education. The real crisis in higher education is older than faddish attention acknowledges; it goes deeper than mere curricular reform can touch.

The problems are simply enough stated. Professionalization within the university has sapped our ability to provide the general education Americans need. For democratic politics to thrive we need a common culture based upon everyone's having access to the means of knowing and understanding. We deny in America not simply a reasonable material equality, but—far more destructively—an equality of dignity and respect. The elite universities especially serve this last inequality. The value of their products—prestige, privilege, power, the appearance of authority—depends upon relative scarcity. If these goods were to become commonly available, they would lose their purchasing power.

The dissolution of requirements in the sixties diminished—in the telling metaphor of many curricular reports—the value of the coin. The market was flooded, as we know, with more holders of the bachelor's degree than could be accommodated. The establishment of a core curriculum is an unconsciously astute solution. The reform is expensive to enact and to maintain; few colleges outside the elite ones will be able to afford it. Thus the coin of some institutions will rise in value at the expense of others.

Derek Bok's 1978 presidential report to the Harvard governing boards and alumni unintentionally reveals what and who a Harvard education actually promotes. President Bok frames his reflections on the state of his university with some remarks about his grandfather, Edward Bok, an archetypically self-made man of the nineteenth century. Edward Bok left school at 13. Later in life he was asked by the Yale *Daily News* if he regretted missing the college experience. His grandson quotes his response with no evident uneasiness about the values expressed: "I cannot picture to myself, much as I should like to do so, the environment of the modern college equipping a man for the practical affairs of life...." The

---

We deny in America not simply a reasonable material equality, but—far more destructively—an equality of dignity and respect. The elite universities especially serve this last inequality.

---

failure of the nineteenth-century college is at least clear: It did not advance a man's business career or add to his money-making abilities. After much commentary intended to demonstrate the self-awareness of the Harvard faculty and the quality of Harvard's liberal education, President Bok returns to his grandfather: "To a boy without money in 1880, college must have seemed an expensive luxury. In today's world, college has become a necessity for young people of talent who aspire to an interesting life and a challenging career." The success of the twentieth-century college is manifest: Its degrees have become prerequisites of material success.

President Bok laments the current atmosphere on campuses as one "tainted" by "pressure, anxiety, and competition for jobs." He believes the problem results from expanding enroll-ments and students' expectations that a college degree would insure "a better job, a larger income, a higher status." A close reader should be puzzled—for what the president at this point regrets is what he himself advances as the purpose of a college education. He places responsibility elsewhere: The number of worthwhile jobs did not expand as rapidly as col-lege enrollments. The disappointment to the hopes of many does not greatly trouble him, for he sees the difficulty work-ing itself out quite naturally: "Students will begin to have more modest expectations...; employers will gradually up-grade jobs to take advantage of the better educated men and women..., and the number of college graduates competing for work will decline" with the drop in the percentage of 18-year-olds. And, one might add, the value of a Harvard diploma will be undiminished, the ranks of privilege maintained.

The report indicates that this implicitly crass justification of worldly success as the primary end of a college education is not simply the president's humor. Bok summarizes 20 years of data on changes in attitudes and aspirations among Har-vard students through the course of their four years. Most notably, students' career ambitions rise, as does their desire for "higher status activities." Apparently in pursuit of these aims, the students achieve "a taste for self-discipline and control combined with a tendency to value achievement and power more highly than relations with other people." Har-vard students agreed, looking back upon their education, that the college had "little influence on present friendships, or on moral, political, or religious perspectives," and "little lasting effect on their moral and ethical views." This evidence would compel most of us to ask the harshest questions about the quality of the liberal education President Bok commends. Instead, he proclaims society's need for generalists, notes that Harvard graduates have "a penchant" for such careers, and apparently assumes that they will somehow be those "in-dividuals who can make decisions that require a sensitivity to many kinds of interests and an understanding of many dif-ferent values and feelings and ways of looking at the world."

Perhaps we are to understand that "generalists" means "power hungry." It would seem that Harvard has no need of a new curriculum, for it has been impressively successful in producing students with the attitudes essential to making money, achieving power, and cloaking their privilege with evasive rhetoric.

The reforms Harvard has adopted are not in themselves wrong. They are too little and too late. They fail even to examine the internal structures in the university responsible for the problems. The immodesty and expense of the process in relation to the result should trouble us. Harvard no longer leads but has come to embody the difficulties that must be overcome if America is to renew its culture. It would be reassuring to believe with the *New York Times* that a first-rate educational institution survives, able to bring unusual intelligence and imagination to its problems. If such an institution exists, it is not Harvard. The Harvard deliberations revealed a depressing resemblance to the efforts of other universities to create new curricula. Whitehead would recognize with sadness what has happened to his Harvard: "The aged are those who, before all things, desire not to make a mistake." We must all share a concern that so many individuals of distinguished mind and achievement have been led to such a mediocre end. The whole process might teach the rest of us engaged in our own searchings for what ought to be done.

We exist in a divided culture. Some have access to the means of understanding; most do not. Higher education will remain fatally compromised unless it confronts the unholy privileges that accompany a degree. Harvard's president is hardly alone in his uncritical acceptance of the university as the principal avenue to power and prosperity in America. We will make no worthy advances until we act out of a realization articulated by the French philosopher Paul Ricoeur: "Every man who thinks and writes, without being hindered in his study or his research in a regime in which his work is negotiated as merchandise, must perceive that his freedom and joy are corrupt, for they are the counterpart and, whether closely or remotely, the condition and the means of work which elsewhere is without freedom and joy...."

For all the expansion of knowledge we know no more than the Greeks or the great Indian philosophers about the knowledge that truly matters. We know nothing more about how to become virtuous human beings, about how to make sane and decent living places for each other, about how to keep from either self-destruction or the destruction of others.

What we need is what we have always needed, and it is rare: great teachers among us. After that we need honest teachers who can acknowledge their ignorance and can join with their students in the efforts to lift it. No system can make great teachers, though some forms of education may present fewer obstacles to such men and women. Graduate education could be designed to encourage honest teachers and to broaden the universe of discourse they inhabit. It is here that general education is desperately needed and everywhere ignored. We now inherit the failures of several generations in higher education. The Harvard curriculum is ample evidence that most scholars and teachers no longer share a common discourse. Knowing that, they have come to rely on our society's substitute for the political and the educated life. Bureaucratic procedure creates the appearance of democracy by eliminating its substance. Some scholars and teachers have escaped the narrowness of their training; some remain always immune to it. It is these few who keep alive what vital education goes on.

IV

A VIEW FROM THE INSIDE

James Q. Wilson

Over the last few years, scores of faculty members, students, and administrators have been involved in the difficult and still unfinished business of trying to reshape a part of the Harvard College curriculum. There is nothing most of us would like better than to be left alone in this enterprise— not because we have no use for criticism, but because we do not see Harvard as a model for what all colleges ought to be. Believing in the virtues of educational diversity, convinced that colleges have begun to acquire a dulling sameness in their curricula, and knowing that what is possible in one place may be (for reasons of tradition, organization, or finances) impossible or undesirable in another, we have avoided issuing manifestos or claiming any special virtue.

But it is not to be: The emerging debate over curricular change has cast Harvard in the role of exemplar, assumed that whatever it did ought to represent the ideal, and criticized it for falling short of that ideal. The nature of that ideal differs, of course, depending on the identity of the critic: Kenneth Lynn, writing in *Commentary*, wishes we had created a more coherent humanistic curriculum based on the great books; Henry Fairlie, in a syndicated column, berates us for not becoming more like an idealized Oxford; Alston

Chase, writing in *Atlantic*, worries that the liberal arts have been so subverted by relativistic social scientists and pandering to student wants as to make any curricular change suspect; and Barry O'Connell, writing in this book, protests that elite colleges perpetuate a social inequality, a tendency likely to be made worse by a core curriculum. Each has his own explanation as to why Harvard should have failed to attain the critic's personal ideal: departmental provincialism, philistine professors, weak administrators, the temper of the times, the rottenness of society, or whatever.

I wish Messrs. Lynn, Fairlie, Chase, and O'Connell had been in the meetings I attended where these matters were discussed. In fact, they *were* there—not in person, of course, but vicariously, for each of these views was ardently and forcefully expressed by one or more professors or students who were part of the Harvard self-examination. Indeed, I expressed some of these opinions myself. Above all, I wish Professors Lynn and O'Connell would suggest what method, other than hand-to-hand combat, they would have employed to decide which of their opposed views of the purposes of higher education ought to prevail. Even that would be too easy, for what was at issue was not simply two conflicting opinions but dozens of conflicts, large and small, in the preferences of the several hundred members of the Faculty of Arts and Sciences who eventually played some role in shaping the final decision.

It would be a mistake, however, to leave matters with the banal statement that change requires compromise, accompanied by a plea for sympathy. For what struck me most forcefully throughout this process was the extent to which there *is* agreement among a majority of the faculty on at least the broad outlines of a core curriculum. Some professors, notably many in the physical sciences, were resolutely opposed to any nondepartmental requirements for the baccalaureate degree, but most believed that general education was a worthwhile objective, that students should be required to obtain an informed acquaintance with certain bodies of knowledge and intellectual skills outside their own special interests, that general education at Harvard had failed in recent years to provide that acquaintance in any coherent manner, and that the time was ripe for rethinking the content of the nondepartmental course offerings.

Even more striking was the amount of agreement on what subjects should be part of a general education requirement. From the report of the Task Force on the Core Curriculum through the final legislation passed by the faculty—a period of nearly two years involving the most intensive and extensive discussions within the faculty—the list of subjects that ought to be part of a core remained pretty much the same: mathematics, natural science, literature, moral philosophy, foreign cultures, social analysis, expository writing. The most significant change was the addition of history as a separate requirement. (It was originally proposed that various courses in other required fields be taught along historical lines.) A foreign language is still required, though the level of prescribed competence has been increased somewhat.

To me, the extent and the durability of the agreement on broad outlines were the most encouraging aspects of an otherwise intense debate. Now the fact that a large number of men and women agree on something does not make that something true or desirable. On the other hand, if no such broad consensus had emerged, no significant curricular change would have been possible in practice or in principle.

Professor O'Connell rightly notes that there is as yet no curriculum in existence; what we have is enabling legislation accompanied by a set of guidelines. The meaning of these will depend on the work of committees now being formed to establish criteria for the designation of courses as meeting the core requirement. He is wrong, however, in suggesting that what is emerging is "mechanical and bureaucratic," the mere proliferation of endless committees, and a "reverence for departmental prerogatives." While an outsider might understandably draw that conclusion from the rather sparse legislation and the announcement of yet more committees, a judgment based on this impression neglects the enormous significance of the process itself and the changed ways of thinking among persons who have been part of that process.

Ten years ago, even five years ago, the Harvard faculty, like the faculties of most colleges, was not inclined to think seriously about undergraduate education. During the tumultuous days of 1969 and 1970, when some students hoped that a by-product of the radical political attack on universities might be a renewed faculty interest in educational issues, the only two curricular decisions made by the Faculty of Arts and Sciences were to recommend the abolition of ROTC and the adoption of an Afro-American studies program. During my 17 years at Harvard, the purposes of an undergraduate education have been rarely, if ever, discussed at faculty meetings or even at the faculty club (politics and the

---

The emerging debate over curricular change has cast Harvard in the role of exemplar, assumed that whatever it did ought to represent the ideal, and criticized it for falling short of that ideal.

Red Sox tend to dominate conversations at the luncheon table). The one or two faculty debates on general education, such as that precipitated in 1964 by the report of a committee headed by Paul Doty, tended to focus on subsidiary issues and to have inconclusive outcomes. During the last two or three years, the faculty, in large groups and small ones, has discussed this question in considerable detail. Though the reaction to the new legislation ranges from apprehensive to enthusistic, there is on all sides a renewed sense that the curriculum is important, that it has been neglected, and that the time is ripe for fresh effort and new ideas.

From afar, all this is hard to discern; even close up it may prove evanescent. Praising an institution for creating an opportunity for change may seem like faint praise indeed, but what is the alternative? Bold anḋ stimulating proposals offered at other universities without protracted and extensive faculty consultation—without, in short, endless committees —went down to defeat. Writing a manifesto is easy; getting others to sign it, vote for it, and live by it is more difficult.

The central problem is this: There have been two academic revolutions, not simply one. The one with which we are all familiar is that described by David Riesman and Christopher Jencks—the transfer of the locus of scholarly loyalty and efforts from the college to the professions. The other is the transfer of power within the universities from trustees and administrators to the faculty. As a result, we have a paradox: The faculty is supposed to govern collegially but it is not a collegium. Once a strong university president may have been able to impose a new curriculum (though even such formidable personages as Charles W. Eliot, James Bryant Conant, and Robert Maynard Hutchins encountered strong resistance). Today, that would be virtually impossible. Once a professor may have thought of his or her primary ties as with colleagues on campus; today, those ties are in large part with colleagues in other states and other countries.

The problem of producing change in a self-governing but externally oriented community is one that every advocate of bolder, tougher, more comprehensive curricular change must face, but I suspect O'Connell must face it in acute form. He criticizes the university from the left, as a bastion of privilege and a source of inequality. Because of its professionalization, its specialization, and its departmentalization, he argues, it resists providing a "common culture," though he does not suggest what this common culture might be or why universities, which have spawned most of the leading critics of our society, should be described as so supportive of that society.

My concern, however, is not with the vague and somewhat rhetorical nature of O'Connell's analysis of society and the place of colleges in it, but rather with the implications of what I take to be his preferred alternative. A society without significant inequalities and organized along communal rather than hierarchical lines would no doubt have certain virtues, but it would also have the defects of those virtues. We have already in our midst a reasonably close approximation of a society where democracy flourishes, inequality is at a minimum, freedom is virtually unfettered, and hierarchy exists only in rudimentary form: the university faculty. The admirable features of a faculty are readily apparent. Individuals are left alone, no one presumes to have the authority to commit someone else to action without that someone's consent; inequalities (at least among the tenured members of the faculty) are slight (even the pay range is much narrower than in other professions); and deans govern more by indulgence than by command. The costs of this form of social organization are no less apparent. Change is slow and requires endless discussion; bold visions of an ideal curriculum are subjected to skeptical scrutiny; coordinated action is difficult to achieve; and the kinds of decisions most easily made by bureaucracies either do not get made at all or are made contingent on their winning a broader acceptance. As President Derek Bok is reported to have said after the faculty vote on the core curriculum proposal, changing a college is like moving a cemetery.

One might rejoin that I have overstated the communal nature of faculty organization. By my own testimony, is not the faculty fragmented into jealously independent departments, representing professional, research, and thus external, interests? Indeed it is so organized, but not with the consequences for curricular change that one might imagine. Departmental power, contrary to O'Connell's assertion, is not the chief impediment to change. The chief impediment to change is beliefs, some of which happen to correspond to departmental or professional loyalties, but others of which are highly individualistic, and all of which are deeply held.

These beliefs concern how one perceives both the broad purposes and the practical details of higher education. One cannot understand the protracted debate within Harvard over the role of natural sciences or foreign languages in a core curriculum by supposing that departmental representatives were simply protecting their turf. Scientists differed as to whether real science can be taught to nonscientists, and whether any science that was taught to nonspecialists should emphasize historical, experimental, or quantitative elements. The departments offering instruction in foreign languages had mixed feelings: They believed such instruction was valuable but worried about whether they ought to shoulder the massive burden of basic instruction in a required language.

The insistence on such instruction came from persons who valued it on intellectual grounds, and they were found (as were their opponents) scattered through many departments. The debate over a requirement in moral philosophy touched not departmental prerogatives but the serious question of whether instruction in such a subject should best proceed along historical, linguistic, or thematic lines. The historians, to be sure, believed that history ought to be included in the core, but neither their arguments nor their votes carried the day. What proved decisive was the endorsement of this view by a biologist, a classicist, and a political scientist.

Motives are usually mixed, and at Harvard there were interests as well as opinions at stake. Every department was concerned lest the creation of a new core curriculum lead to the appointment of faculty members without departmental review and recommendations. Some departments worried about the budgetary implications of seeing enrollments in introductory courses soar or collapse depending on whether such courses did or did not receive core designation. And no department is likely to feel comfortable about the management of the core program if it is entirely unrepresented on the various committees charged with that management. But I believe it fair to say that at no point in the deliberations were these strictly organizational and departmental concerns of decisive significance, or even of very great importance. As is so often the case when matters of fundamental consequence are at stake, ideas rather than interests tend to prevail.

I do not know whether the effort to revitalize general (that is, liberal arts) education will succeed. Harvard is, at best, at the end of the beginning, not the beginning of the end. The contrary pressures are enormous. The rate of increase in the money resources of the university has slowed to the point that new funds will have to be found just to stay even, to say nothing of moving ahead. If, as many social scientists believe, organizational change usually requires the availability of slack resources, then even the richest college is in trouble. The altered conditions of the labor market mean that Harvard is reemphasizing liberal arts education at the very moment when student demand for preprofessional and occupational training is rising. Finally, the United States is committed to mass higher education on a scale unrivaled in the world. (If O'Connell cavils at the elitism of American universities, what would he say of England, France, or Germany?) The increase in enrollment has so expanded the size and diversity of the student body and faculty of a typical college as to make the task of defining and defending curricular requirements far harder than before, when a small number of persons of similar social background took courses from professors numbered in the dozens rather than the hundreds.

But there are some favorable tendencies as well. The near collapse of the market for new PhDs has led to substantial cuts in graduate students enrollments, with two potentially desirable effects: Less faculty time need be spent on graduate teaching fellows; more faculty time may have to be spent on undergraduates.

But the shifting balance of resources and constraints only sets the outer limits on what may be done. Ultimately, everything depends, as O'Connell notes, on the existence of good teachers—decent, cultivated, stimulating men and women. Their supply is limited and cannot be readily expanded; indeed, I suspect there are, proportionately, as many today, in an era of research, as there ever were in a supposedly halcyon past. No curricular designs, whether those Harvard has made explicit or those O'Connell leaves implicit, are likely to change that.

V

ISSUES AND PROBLEMS
A DEBATE*

with Louis Benezet, Joel Conarroe, Jewel P. Cobb,
Phyllis Keller, Robert E. Marshak, John Ratté, Henry
Rosovsky, Frederick Rudolph, Edward G. Sparrow, Ilja
Wachs, Henry R. Winkler.

Henry Rosovsky and Phyllis Keller: It is often said that
our present dissatisfaction with what goes on in higher education stems from the campus upheavals of the late 1960s and
faculty capitulation to student demands for free educational
choice. But the problem of collegiate education today derives
from much longer-term social and intellectual trends. By and
large, faculties abolished requirements (spurred, to be sure,
by student activists) because they themselves were no longer
sure of the rationale for them.

For most of this century, the proportion of young people
completing high school and entering college has risen stead-
ily. By the 1960s about half of the college-age cohort was
entering some kind of postsecondary educational institution.
The extraordinary size of the college population simply made
more vivid the fact that no other country in the world has attempted to provide higher education for its citizenry on so
massive a scale. As its mass increased, so did the heterogeneity of the student population. Student diversity—in level of
preparation, background, interests, and abilities—as much as
size placed older assumptions about the nature of higher ed-

* Debate based on a Colloquium sponsored by the Council on Academic Affairs of The
College Board.

ucation under great pressure.

The postwar era also saw important intellectual ⌐nd institutional change: the explosive growth of knowledge—in quantity, diversity, and difficulty; the expanded research function of the university and the ever closer identification of faculty members with their disciplines and their professional activities; mounting pressure on students to undertake technical and professional studies at the earliest possible time. These changes made the older model of a broad and unified liberal arts education seem anachronistic. Institutions of higher learning took on an extraordinary range of functions; faculty no less than students demanded freedom to pursue their own interests with minimal constraint.

To a large extent, curricular and other reforms in recent years reflected these pressures. There was a growing sense that all restrictions were arbitrary, that all student choices, all faculty offerings were of equal merit. Liberal education lost touch with its root meaning as a form of intellectual training and became bound up with issues of political liberty (or freedom of choice) and emotional development.

By the 1970s, the majority of faculties in most liberal arts colleges were unhappy with this new status quo, but they were uncertain about how to change it. Their traditional aversion to vocational training at the undergraduate level remained intact. No less disquieting was the intellectual parochialism and mis- (or non-) education that often seemed to be the result of unfettered student choice. But many doubted the possibility of achieving agreement on a new standard for liberal education.

The older rationale held that the primary purpose of a college education is to provide general knowledge and develop intellectual capacities such as independent reasoning, understanding, and judgment. At Harvard we take the view that these goals remain as central as ever and that the three conventional components of the curriculum—general requirements, a field of concentration, and electives—provide the best framework for achieving them.

The growth of intellectual specialization has strengthened

the position of individual disciplines. Students and faculty
more than ever define themselves in terms of their special
subjects (sociology, biology, English, etc.). Similarly, the
laissez-faire impulse of recent years has given a special cachet
to free electives. But the idea of general education—a set of
courses reflecting some central and common agreement on
essentials—has badly eroded.

In the course of its recent review of undergraduate education, the Harvard faculty took a fresh look at the character
and interrelationship of the traditional parts of the curriculum and decided to set out on the complex and difficult
task of creating a core offering comparable in importance to
the disciplinary major and electives.

In most (but not all: Chicago and Columbia are among the
honorable exceptions) liberal arts colleges today, the
equivalent of the core or general education component of the
curriculum is a distribution requirement: a numerical formula
specifying that students take at least a couple of courses in
each of the major areas of knowledge—humanities, social
sciences, and natural sciences. We take the view that such a
loose sampling among departmental courses is unlikely to
foster the intellectual breadth that is part of what college is all
about. Yet an evenhanded introduction to all fields of learning is no longer possible. What is needed is a coherent principle that directs students specifically and selectively to the
knowledge, skills, and habits of thought that (in the view of
the faculty) seem now to be of general and lasting value.

In tackling this task, the Harvard faculty sought to
establish a standard of liberal learning to be met by all
students. This does not imply that students need take an identical set of courses, nor master a single set of great books. The
faculty concluded that:

> our goal is to encourage a critical appreciation of and in-
> formed acquaintance with the major *approaches* to
> knowledge, not in abstract but in substantive terms, so
> that students have an understanding of what kinds of
> knowledge exist in certain important areas, how such
> knowledge is acquired, how it is used, and what it might
> mean to them personally. We seek, in other words, to

have students acquire basic literacy in major forms of intellectual discourse.

It is sometimes argued that this is essentially a remedial approach to higher education and that Harvard students in particular have little need of it. But the fact is that even a student body chosen on the basis of outstanding abilities and achievements is unlikely to have reached this standard prior to college. Furthermore, the understanding that the core tries to provide is not something learned once and for all, but ideally is reinforced and enriched at every stage of learning: in primary and secondary school, in college, in professional or graduate school, and in the experience of life and career thereafter.

To this end, the Harvard faculty fashioned requirements in five key areas. Literature and Arts requirements will acquaint students with important literary and artistic achievements and aim also to foster a critical appreciation of major forms of artistic expression. Historical study will focus on the significant aspects of the present world viewed in historical perspective and will attempt to demonstrate the complexity of particular events that have shaped a portion of history irreversibly. Requirements in social analysis and moral reasoning will examine major concepts in social science and moral and political philosophy and will develop students' abilities to think systematically about fundamental aspects of contemporary society and about recurring questions of choice and value. A science requirement will acquaint students with basic principles of the physical, biological, and behavioral sciences and with science as a way of looking at man and the world. A foreign cultures requirement is designed to expand students' range of cultural experiences and to provide fresh perspectives on their own values, assumptions, and traditions.

In addition, standards of competence must be met in expository writing, mathematics, and foreign languages. These are viewed as basic intellectual tools that provide access to studies throughout the curriculum.

The core areas are related to each other by a common question: What are knowledge and understanding, and how are they acquired and applied? That different ways of looking at the universe, society, and ourselves overlap to some degree is no disadvantage but rather reflects the true state of learning, with its ever-shifting boundaries. In this sense the core is not only a sector of the curriculum with its own reason for being but serves also as an entry (and a buttress) to the student's work in his or her major and electives.

While the core takes a broad view of the areas of learning, concentrations explore a particular field in depth. By penetrating more or less deeply into that field, the student can (or at least ought to) get to the point where he or she can compare and criticize authorities, summon evidence to the test of theory, construct alternative explanations, see not

---

The laissez-faire impulse of recent years has given a special cachet to free electives. But the idea of general education—a set of courses reflecting some central and common agreement on essentials—has badly eroded.

---

merely facts but the possibilities of further facts—and so in general attain a modest but real degree of intellectual autonomy.

Electives ideally add to that autonomy. They allow some students to achieve greater depth in concentration, others to be dilettantes in the good sense—to choose and to explore simply to take delight (or find rest and rehabilitation from more strenuous intellectual endeavors) in a variety of subjects. Free choice unadorned can be as debilitating and mind destroying as complete constraint; in combination with the generalized discipline supplied by the core and the specialized discipline provided by the major, it becomes an essential avenue to the self-development that is the real goal of education.

The distinctive feature of Harvard's curriculum reform is that it tries to adapt timeless values of liberal education to current intellectual and social realities. The growth of knowledge and its ever more important role in the organization of society may be deplored by those who yearn for a simpler world. But it is real; it is here; it will not go away. Higher education in the late twentieth century must rethink what it means to "provide general knowledge and to develop general intellectual capacities." The heterogeneity of the student population poses a different kind of problem, for it suggests both the importance of establishing a standard and the need to accommodate differences of interest and ability within the standard.

But while these new realities require a change in strategy, the essential intellectual and social aims of liberal education remain the same. Indeed, the primary social task of American colleges and universities—insuring the survival of democratic values by the creation of an educated citizenry capable of making intelligent and responsible choices—is more crucial, and a greater challenge, than ever before.

Henry R. Winkler: The new core curriculum proposed at Harvard is important, if only because of the public relations value of anything that comes out of the greatest of our universities. But it may be important only for that reason. Most college and university faculties are once again seeking greater curricular coherence in undergraduate education and a summary definition of what we mean by an educated person. But some never quite retreated into the chaos of the cafeteria style of free election that characterized the late 1950s and 1960s.

Both my children were at Harvard between 1962 and 1970. They chose somewhat different areas of concentration but, for the life of me, I couldn't see what patterns of educational philosophy emerged from the random selection of courses that paraded across the computer printouts that signaled their progress. I could see little evidence that the Harvard faculty, so distinguished in countless areas of specialized research, was giving any serviceable attention to the purpose and the special requirements of baccalaureate education. For that reason alone, I'm grateful that the faculty has again addressed such questions. In contrast, many institutions, like the College of Arts and Sciences in my own present university, retained much more shape to the curriculum. They insisted upon an English language requirement, continued to believe that there was some value to achieving competence in a foreign language, and in general remained wedded to the system of concentration and distribution that had been the national norm for quite some time.

I am sympathetic to the point of view expressed in Harvard's definition of a core, and indeed I am aware of the dangers of maximalist thinking. But I am troubled about the almost unlimited choice mandated by the Harvard faculty, so that in reality (with some differences, of course) we have a return to older distribution requirements much more loosely structured than in many other institutions. The program seems as much concerned with faculty turf and territory as those of any of the less prestigious institutions. It is still light-years away, for example, from the old University of Chicago general education program, the erosion of which marked an unfortunate retreat. The reasons are complicated and they are not all educational. All of us are concerned about the need for a commitment to bring structure and some unity to liberal undergraduate education. Of course, there are good things in the core curriculum. Historians must applaud recognition of the need for a historical orientation to present events and a historical perspective on the past. But even here, is one thing really as important for undergraduates as another? Thus, despite the definitions, I read the Harvard core curriculum to say that my own quite specialized work in twentieth-century British politics and diplomacy might be elected, since it fulfills the definitions outlined in the Harvard report section on historical process and perspectives. And I am not at all convinced, whatever the rhetoric, that tossing a series of such courses into a grab bag of selection is to create some cohesive approach to the past of a kind that is so lacking in our singularly present-minded society.

Undergraduate education needs a thorough overhaul, not just a few Band-Aids applied here and there. It's still highly segmented, still rigidly locked into the tiny compartments that represent the particular way each of us finds toward specialized knowledge. Our students, and not just those at Harvard, have rightly complained about the barriers, even when they had little perception of the mode and importance of searching out specialized knowledge. Attempts to break down those barriers have often foundered upon the rocks of superficiality and artificiality. But few of us have done much to foster those exchanges that might encourage student motivation and inquiry and to promote the notion that our

---

I am troubled about the almost unlimited choice mandated by the Harvard faculty, so that in reality we have a return to older distribution requirements much more loosely structured than in many other institutions.

—Henry R. Winkler

---

compartmentalized offerings might not always be the adequate or the proper ways to stimulate effective undergraduate learning.

Does the Harvard plan move us further along the road to that kind of coherence and new synthesis that appears to me so desperately needed? To a certain extent, yes. Some special, newly thought through, and presumably integrative courses are proposed as part of the core. But then there are so many concessions to the vested interests of discrete departments, so much of what appears to be rationalization to insure that most departments get a piece of the action, that the value of rethinking the curriculum may well have been eroded. The Harvard faculty has every advantage of resources, of stable enrollment, of leadership that most of our institutions don't enjoy. If that faculty can come up with no more than a partial and patchwork reconstitution of what was done 40 years ago, how do other faculties manage to transcend special interests and self-serving myopia in a time of declining enrollments, declining budgets, and declining jobs? It's a difficult challenge. One really wonders whether it is being faced.

Louis Benezet: I find myself torn between congratulating Dean Rosovsky and his faculty on an attempt to restore the curriculum of a great university to a truly liberalized concept and a great howl over the fact that most of the publicity has described this as a different or new kind of general education. This sounds like a semantic quibble, but, unfortunately, it has a way of confusing people so that they find themselves talking about the wrong issue, namely, what knowledge is of most worth and who should be worthy to have it. I will display my bias at once; the real question is: How do people become educated and what must be expected of them? And this is the greatest lack that I find in reading the curriculum proposals from Harvard. Liberal education is a well-domesticated concept, comfortable at all faculty luncheons. It has a 2500-year tradition, beginning with Socrates and going through John Henry Newman, Alexander Meikeljohn, Ortega y Gasset, and so on.

At the same time, every professor will tell you that he is an exponent of liberal education, no matter what he is teaching. Amherst President William Ward said that any teacher knows that the intensive pursuit of a particular question will carry one far beyond the conventional compartmentalized definition of a subject. Now this is liberal education slightly romanticized but also highly graspable by anybody who wants to teach anything. Where we remain confused is in how to apply it—what is to be taught, what is to be taken by the students, and what the students are expected to do to make the most of their study.

General education, I maintain, remains in itself an unpopular subject. It is a kind of blue-collar idea. It also thinly disguises the fact that too many of us, perhaps, think that too many people are going to college anyway and that general education is some kind of diet that is consumable by the multitudes, or that it is what you talk about when you have to apologize for the fact that real education is not consumable by the people. The subject of general education does not disguise the fact, as I see it, that meritocracy is in the saddle in our education more strongly today than at any time since World War II.

I don't think that any conversation about the new curriculum at Harvard or anywhere else is going to change things until this other debate is resolved by the faculty itself. General education remains unpopular with them. It suggests that some students are not fit to take the rigorous stuff that enables a professor to replicate himself in his students—the ultimate good. General education also implies that any professor should be ready to take a crack at anything. Obviously, that is anti-intellectual. It implies that college professors should try to teach almost any subject within reasonable distance of their own competence, whatever that may be. And this, in itself, implies a sort of *mea culpa* about specialization and expertise. Needless to say, that is not a favorite faculty pose. Thus, these questions remain to be resolved before we can expect a program, whether you call it liberal education or general education, to make real changes in what happens dynamically with a college or university curriculum. If a faculty of Harvard's eminence is to change attitudes toward general education among the students, as well as among the public, I doubt that this will be brought about by official direction committees (whether chaired by the dean or by his surrogates) that set out to advise academic departments. It takes time; it takes persistence; it takes constant willingness to face defeat and being outmaneuvered by words. A solid year, perhaps three, has been required on most campuses for any dent to be made in attitudes toward teaching something other than one's specialty and calling it liberal education and, therefore, fit for any kind of student curriculum.

To get out of this trap I suggest that we might look at several things: To begin with, when a program is written by 50 people, you don't have a camel, you have a whole circus. And somebody has to face the fact that if general education is to be more than the glorification of one's own specialty, faculty development for general education is required. You've got to convince faculty that there are other ways of approaching subject matter than the particular niche from which they come.

The other matter that bothers me about this eminently desirable program is that the students scarcely appear at all. And this is rather curious: not only because the students are paying a considerable bill, but because they are not the students of 40 years ago. They have been places; they have read; they have criticized; some of them have even voted. They have things to contribute to their education. They want to contribute. The students want part of the action; they want to react; they want to be in on the making of the subject matter, as well as the consumption of it.

And this leads to my closing concerns and the philosophy of the program as I grasp it. It seems still bound by a teacher-centered idea that knowledge and understanding issue from a professor's mouth or from a laboratory report or from a textual reference. Is this truly knowledge, or is it the material from which the student's knowledge and understanding gradually emerge as he or she processes this material on the basis of personal experience and emotions and needs?

Jewel Cobb: As we plan the education of our students for the eighties, there are six points I wish to make: (1) Beyond the basic skills of reading, writing, and mathematics, the foundation of common knowledge should focus on the processes or methodology of the discipline and on problem solving. Then the content flows with meaning and motivation. For the student this changes the psychology of the curriculum from one of required courses to achievement goals; i.e., this is what I want to achieve. This is how the historian works. I discovered only recently that a historian is a detective, seeking and searching for clues and developments of literal truths in a step-by-step logical process. I thought, somehow, from my unfortunate and poor teaching, that history consisted of dates and the development of ideas that were more or less to be memorized. I did not know the excitement of the process of the historian in developing the facts. I only learned "memorized" facts. Somehow we missed that, at least some of us. And so the style of the teacher is extremely important.

(2) The knowledge explosion, diverse faculty viewpoints, and the territoriality of disciplines make faculty committee decisions about course content a formidable task. But this approach of asking what do we want to achieve may help us move to some kind of consensus about courses and the broad knowledge base that all students ought to have. Definitely, as is indicated in the Harvard plan, new syllabi must be written for many integrated, interdisciplinary courses. But this will take considerable planning and faculty coordination, plus a little genie with money around to release faculty so that they can get on with this very important task. There also must be umbrella courses, covering four to five courses. They have yet to be written. They must not be simply "an introduction to" courses. The knowledge explosion demands that this be done. And here again, the instructor is the important factor in bringing these new courses to fruition.

(3) If an institution says that an assigned body of knowledge is the only way to implement goals, then that curriculum should constitute no more than 20 to 25 percent of the courses needed for the degree. We must leave as many unassigned credits as possible for the student's creative choice in electives, since the work in the subject of the major is also important. Nervous parents and nervous students often see preparation in the major as essential for an immediate vocation or further graduate or professional school work.

(4) We must not forget that the student body of today is different from the student group in the 1940s and 1950s. Now there are over 43 percent—over 4.5 million—women in traditional colleges. And there are over 11 percent or 800,000 plus minority students, as first-time students in college, excluding

the counts of continuing education and adult students. Our deliberations should in some measure be cognizant of what they—women and minorities—bring to the classroom. To ignore scholarly contributions already made by these two groups is to state that they are invisible and, therefore, irrelevant. This is a hidden agenda that we do not want to convey as educators.

(5) We must be certain that we are not falling into an educational version of a law-and-order mentality. We hear the word "standards"—slipping of standards, wobbly standards. The question we must ask is: Are the grading criteria of the faculty changing? If so, that is the professor's problem. Expectations for quality performance should persist in the

---

If a faculty of Harvard's eminence is to change attitudes toward general education among the students, as well as among the public, I doubt that this will be brought about by official direction committees that set out to advise academic departments.

—Louis Benezet

---

classroom. But are we trying to keep students out or are we trying to bring them in to learn? It is a most unrealistic time to close the gates just when high school populations are going down. In the 1980s, there will be fewer students in the pool and they must see our curriculum as attractive and not as an obstacle course. (6) I might say something about the goals and the outcomes of a liberal education from the human perspective: We hope these young graduates will emerge less provincial and more tolerant of other cultures, with a global perspective, a one-world concept; that as they move through their college years clear thinking will help them to eliminate all vestiges of sexism and racism. They will graduate less angry, we hope, and therefore more rational and more analytical, more able to cope with the unknown. Lastly, we wish to educate improved citizens. At the moment, only one third of eligible 18-year-olds cast their votes.

Robert Marshak: City College has always served the children of the poor, the immigrant, and the disadvantaged. Thus it has, from its inception, combined the requirements of general education with a concern for career training. The founder of City College, Townsend Harris, stated in 1847 that "while it shall be in no way inferior to any of our colleges in the character or amount of value of the information given to the pupils, the courses of study to be pursued will have more special reference to the active duties of life."

Throughout its much shorter history, "proletarian Harvard" has attempted to develop curricula geared to the practical needs of its students as well as to the intellectual demands of the age. In line with this tradition, City College in 1977 replaced a very permissive distribution approach to general education with two core curricula tracks. We couldn't settle on one, so there are two. Core A is less adventurous and simply mandates a reduced menu of departmental offerings within the distribution mode. Core B is a truly innovative, multidisciplinary general education core of 10 semester-long courses. Three of the ten courses in Core B are grouped under the title Man and Nature, and I'd say both the biological and physical sciences have to be represented, in contrast to the Harvard core curriculum.

The other seven courses in this core are language and communication; literature in the human experience; the arts: understanding and experience; world civilizations and cultures; individual, world, and society; political economy; and realities of urban America. If you compare these titles with the Harvard core curriculum, I think you will find a rather good correspondence, except that these are specific multidisciplinary courses; there is not going to be any permissiveness beyond the determination of the content of these courses. In my view, the City College Core B curriculum goes further than the Harvard core curriculum in providing general education for students that, quoting the Harvard prospectus, "will meet the needs of the late twentieth century."

If we agree that higher education can be the most effective instrument for social change in our times, then the general education core must include prescribed courses which sensitize our students to the urban afflictions of postindustrial society and the pressing global problems of human survival. The core curriculum must also reflect a willingness on the part of the faculty, quoting Eric Ashby, "to reconcile the intellectual detachment essential for good scholarship with the social concern essential for the good life." The Harvard core curriculum stops just a little short of fully accepting these challenges, whereas the City College Core B curriculum is attempting to do just that. Perhaps it is a case of fools rushing in where angels fear to tread, but I do not think so.

There is a further objective of the Core B curriculum at City College. We are embarking on a series of programs with substantial foundation funding entitled Liberal Arts, Preprofessional Studies and Public Policy (LAPP). These are intended to restore the liberal arts to a central role in undergraduate education without sacrificing the ultimate career needs of our economically underprivileged student body. The Core B curriculum will provide the starting point for the LAPP programs—preprofessional clusters of courses in the junior and senior years for emerging careers in fields such as communications, mass media and public policy, public policy and public service, energy, ecology and environment, health, medicine and society, and so on. Students in all of the LAPP programs will join in a senior capstone course in public policy and human values which will raise the ethical and social questions that they will face as professionals.

The combination of the Core B curriculum, a preprofessional cluster, the senior capstone course on public policy and human values, plus certain electives, which define a LAPP program, should help educate persons, to quote Ashby, "who can innovate, improvise, solve problems with no precedent."

No general core curriculum worth its salt will succeed, however, without pooling disciplinary faculty talents to hack out the interdisciplinary wisdoms that illuminate the basic methodologies, conceptual frameworks, and value systems of the major areas of human knowledge. The information explosion that has taken place during the last several decades, and the dominant role enjoyed by American universities in worldwide research and scholarship, pose additional barriers to the design of a multidisciplinary core curriculum. Success will come only through concerted efforts to retrain faculty for this mode of teaching and to establish new paths of credentialing (possibly revival of the Doctor of Arts degree), so that young generalists can join the faculty ranks. I personally believe that this great task is worth undertaking.

Frederick Rudolph: Flexibility, uncertainty, mystery, unexpected revelations, love, intuition confirmed by experience, consciousness of one's vulnerability as a human being: This, I suspect we will all agree, is what liberal learning is about. Liberal learning is a style, not a formula. Its goals are not new. Surely it's a good idea to know how to venture into the street and get to the other side alive and to know how to converse on reasonably equal terms with a computer. It's surely a good idea to be able to confront a word and know what it means and to employ it with grace and clarity and perhaps even push it toward new meaning; and to understand that one is a product of the past, a creature of the future, and, at the same time, to recognize oneself as a unique expression of the experience of being human; to be reminded that, while thinking places great demands on the mind and body and makes possible an orderly world, it is but one of the processes that define a human being. It is important to acknowledge that one is born, wherever that may be, in the provinces and that life is an endless challenge to move beyond that particular province, and to live with imagination, wonder, and a delight in the possibilities that inhere in being human.

It is a good idea to understand the nature of the flaws, their sources and their fatal attraction, that define the character of

Richard Nixon. Liberal learning should prepare us to know a good man or a good woman when we see one. Whether these goals can best be achieved through a core of required courses, by an emphasis on content or on form, by a concern with depth or breadth or both is, of course, what curricula planners have always argued over, and I trust always will.

It seems to me, however, that to allow the current interest in the so-called core at Harvard to be distorted into a movement is to deflect energies and resources from tackling more pressing questions for most institutions. For instance, does the curriculum pay attention—enough attention—to the creative capacities and esthetic values of what it means to be human? Does the American academic style place too great an

---

No general core curriculum worth its salt will succeed, however, without pooling disciplinary faculty talents to hack out the interdisciplinary wisdoms that illuminate the basic methodologies, conceptual frameworks, and value systems of the major areas of human knowledge.
—Robert Marshak

---

emphasis on teaching and not enough on learning? Has television reared a generation or generations of students whose judgments are shaped by the values of entertainment, salesmanship, and promotion and, if so, what do we do about it? Is academic leadership so preoccuppied in a kind of unacknowledged warfare with government over accounting practices, admissions, hiring, tenure, sidewalks, and elevators that the essential nature of the enterprise is being neglected?

Without meaning to be an ungracious guest, let me simply ask whether describing the core curriculum as the paramount current issue in higher education may not be helping to deflect our colleges and universities from the really tough questions.

Henry Rosovsky: I read many curriculum reform proposals and I find that they often begin with high-minded philosophy and then you turn the page and they talk about where to put the water coolers in the corridors. What is missing is the in-between. Now the in-between—the concrete and specific statement of educational goals at the level of individual courses—is absolutely essential. One can talk endlessly about coherence and new syntheses. One can rail at departments. But it won't get us anywhere because, you see, the way to make progress is to work with what one can change. It is quite pointless, it seems to me, to sit around and berate what we cannot change. Even if I should wish to, I cannot get rid of departments at Harvard University. President Winkler will not get rid of the departments at the University of Cincinnati, and Dean Cobb won't do it at her institution. The fact is that departments exist for good or ill, and I think that it is a much better idea to work with them rather than to talk against them and get no place. I realize that I have not approached this with sufficient ideological purity; I have heard that criticism before.

Let me now address some of the specific points. President Winkler's comment that Harvard's core curriculum is a simple distribution requirement is just wrong. The essence of a distribution requirement is to set up certain categories: to require, for example, two English courses and three French courses. We have gone much beyond that and have designated specific courses. Yet he accuses us of permitting too much choice. I think that we must be doing something right because we are continually under attack from both sides, either for being too rigid or for being too loose. I don't think there is excessive flexibility when in each one of these areas we will offer students a choice of one out of eight courses—all of which are shaped by the same guidelines and serve the same educational purpose. I disagree a little bit with President Marshak. I don't think that one must include economics per se. That's part of the City College core. Ours includes a requirement in social analysis which can be met by courses presenting the central theories or analytical approaches (and empirical data) of anthropology, sociology, or political science as well as economics.

Dr. Benezet asks who the students were who accused me of putting them in a straitjacket. Let me say first that there was a group of about 35 students who worked very closely, over a long period of time, with various planning and review committees. As a result of their input a number of changes were made in our original proposals. Some other students, acting as individuals, took the view that freedom of choice overrode all other considerations of educational policy. The student press was generally opposed to us from the beginning. That gave me a lot of heart, because I felt that I was probably doing something right. But you might draw a different conclusion.

Robert Marshak: The universities can now be the most effective instrument for social change because we have about 10 million students in attendance who are at the period of their lives when they are very sensitive to the generation of new values. But the question is how much of the hard work of developing these core courses will be done by the faculty themselves. I would hope that the Harvard leadership in this connection would provide an impetus for some major workshops, conferences, and so on, so that faculty who are interested can be retrained to undertake the difficult job.

Henry Rosovsky: One encouraging thing about this whole effort is that many Harvard professors have volunteered to develop new courses and to teach in the core program. I think that in all of our universities there are now many people between 45 and 55 years of age who are tired of teaching more and more about narrower subjects to empty classrooms. Whether they call it general education, liberal education, or a core doesn't matter, but they are looking for an opportunity to deal with something of more general significance at the undergraduate level. The signs are very encouraging judging by the number of courses that faculty have volunteered to fit into this program.

Louis Benezet: This is not unique. I may say that most programs of core curricula—and there are dozens, even hundreds across the country—do get that kind of enthusiasm. What we don't know is what happens six months later, after the classroom door has closed. People have a tendency to revert to what they have been taught to teach, to know, and to disseminate. I still would argue, in the friendliest and most encouraging spirit, that it takes a considerable amount of time for a faculty to agree to make changes in themselves and in the way they approach their entire job. It isn't just a matter of volunteering. It's a matter of retooling oneself, and often of unlearning the things that one has learned for the past 20 to 30 years.

Henry R. Winkler: Obviously all of us work within the realm of what is possible and what can be done, and we do our best to persuade and to learn from each other. But I raise the question as to whether an institution such as mine, or such as Harvard, is going to be in the forefront of curricular redesign, generating the new thinking about undergraduate education that I judge is required. I suspect that some of the smaller liberal arts colleges, because their faculty concentrate on questions of this kind, are likely to be more vital, to give us more leadership in this area than any of our institutions.

Edward Sparrow: I'm the dean at St. John's College in Annapolis. Perhaps most of you know a little bit about that college. It started with Robert Hutchins's idea, and that idea was subsequently translated, through the efforts of Stringfellow Barr and Scott Buchanan, into a required liberal arts program in Annapolis and, later, in Santa Fe. Mr. Rosovsky speaks of a core, but I'd like to know a little bit about what is needed beyond a core: that is to say, the area of concentration or major. I'm quite convinced that the major concentration was not born of the necessities of careers or further professional work. In itself it is thought part of a liberal education. I read in Dean Rosovsky's report that for Harvard cumulative learning is an effective way to develop a student's powers of

reasoning and analysis. I'd like to ask: If the purpose of concentration and a major is to develop a student's powers of
reasoning and analysis, is Harvard's the best way to pursue
that end? There is some experience, at St. John's and
elsewhere, that will say that there are far better ways to pursue that same end.

Henry Rosovsky: Your question illustrates an important
point. I think that American colleges are necessarily and ap-
propriately diverse. They can and should have different goals
and different ways of achieving similar goals. For example,
some colleges gear their programs to vocational training in
nursing or accounting or business, while others emphasize
liberal education. I believe that there are alternative paths to
liberal education; St. John's and Harvard are good examples
of very different models. I do not think that we could mount
the kind of undergraduate program that you have developed
so successfully, nor do I think that you could emulate our
program. In some ways, I might have been very happy with a
St. John's education. But my own experience leads me to
believe that there is great value in going deeply into a field of
knowledge. Furthermore, everything is a trade-off. Your curriculum provides certain benefits at certain costs, and so does
ours. What is most important is that we have both identified
our goals and stated how we mean to achieve them so that
students can make their own choices. The fact that your program is good does not necessarily mean that ours is less good;
it is simply different. We live in a pluralistic society and I
think that our educational system properly reflects that
characteristic.

Ilja Wachs: We have no required curriculum whatever and
the only requirement we make is that a student commit himself or herself deeply, fully, imaginatively, and morally to the
work he or she performs. On the other side, the faculty
member must subordinate his own involvement with the par-
ticularity of his discipline, at least to the extent that he can
imagine the student, his or her needs, resources, and learning

impediments. I don't mean to offer this as a curricular model or a set of assumptions to all institutions. But I am very much struck, as Professor Rudolph was, by the absence in this document of any thought about students that transcends the curricular level. There is no imagination of students in this document. There is no imagination of the particular current cultural and human circumstances under which they come to institutions of higher learning.

There is no imagination, for example, that at this point most middle-class students come to college with an inordinate degree of anxiety about a shrinking marketplace and deal with the subject of their courses instrumentally rather than directly as a consequence of that anxiety. I wonder, in

---

If the purpose of concentration and a major is to develop a student's powers of reasoning and analysis, is Harvard's the best way to pursue that end?

—Edward Sparrow

---

general, whether curricular reform, seen as the major instrument by which institutions of higher education make positive changes, may not to some extent be a diversion. I, too, have known many men and women who have graduated from Harvard, though not my children. When they consistently voice some feeling of being lost, I'm not sure that it comes from an incoherent Chinese menu curriculum. It seems to me to arise because the institution has not fully adopted the ethos of vital, concrete teaching where an imagination of student needs and of student potentialities and possibilities is its real function.

Henry Rosovsky: Let me say first that the curriculum was only one focal point of a very broad review of undergraduate education conducted at Harvard over the last few years. At the same time we also reexamined admissions policies, advising, college life outside the classroom, teaching practices, concentrations, and the deployment of educational resources. It would be foolish to argue that curricular reform is *the* major instrument for effecting positive change. But we found that the curriculum, or rather the general education portion of the curriculum, was in greatest need of improvement. Since the other influences on undergraduate education seemed (with a few minor exceptions) to be operating as well as one might hope, we followed the adage that if it isn't broken, you don't fix it.

I would make two other points. I know as well as anyone else that students are individuals with unique needs and potentialities. And I know that the years from 18 to 22 are terribly important for social and psychological, as well as for intellectual, development. But we cannot *teach* balance and maturity; we can only set examples of these values and create an environment congenial to their growth. What we can teach is how to think clearly and cogently. Whether all students would agree with me, I cannot say; but I would argue that this is one of the most important of student needs.

Finally, a word about advising and its relationship to the curriculum. I can conceive of a system of advising that would be superior to a structured or standardized curriculum, but I think it is impossible to achieve in a large institution. On a per capita basis, I believe that Harvard puts more resources into advising than any other school in the country. And yet we still need to build a certain amount of guidance into the curriculum. Furthermore, you must not overlook the fact that requirements are binding on faculty as well as students; if students have to take certain kinds of courses, then the faculty has to offer them. No system of advising can affect the character of course offerings.

Now as I have said before, the big university colleges are not for everybody. They are for certain types of students. You've got to take Harvard for what it is. We have a faculty that is highly research oriented, absorbed in its own work, interested in the very best students, not very maternalistic, perhaps cold in some ways. All of that may be true. But that's also the glory of the place. For some students it provides the best possible undergraduate experience; for others it can be a mistaken choice. I have no doubt that this is true of other types of schools as well.

Joel Conarroe: Harvard has enormous influence and for this reason I am particularly interested in what Harvard intends to do about the study of foreign languages. This is one of the serious problems facing American education right now. I read through the material and was slightly encouraged, but I find the present statement a little fuzzy. It seems to ask for a kind of reading requirement, but surely no man or woman should be graduated from Harvard who is unable to speak at least one language other than English. You said in your opening statements, Dean Rosovsky, that you want to stiffen up the requirements. Would you comment on what sort of requirements you see as an ideal, and would you say a word about why you think these requirements are essential?

Henry Rosovsky: The language statement was fuzzy because we had not really resolved it. We've always had a language proficiency requirement. But everybody recognizes that it's pegged at a very low level of competence. It certainly doesn't guarantee either reading or speaking ability. My own view is that a merely nominal language requirement is indefensible. In any event, at the time of the core curriculum debates the question of the appropriate level of the requirement and the proper balance between reading and speaking skills was deferred for later consideration. That consideration is now under way. In the interim, what we have done is this: For our Foreign Cultures requirement we've offered students the choice of studying a Western or a non-Western culture. The Western option entails the use of a foreign language, either in lectures or reading assignments. Since we cannot expect any significant number of students to know exotic languages such as Chinese, Japanese, Arabic, etc., the study of non-Western cultures will depend on translations. We hope that the Western option will encourage students who do have language skills to keep them alive in the course of their college studies.

I would like to see the students come to us better prepared in languages. I share the view that we are in danger of becoming a monolingual country in an increasingly interdependent and multilingual world. The high schools can do a great deal to avert this danger but I fear that they are being discouraged by the abandonment of language requirements in American colleges. This latter trend also has a disastrous effect on graduate education. I find that there are fewer and fewer

---

I would like to see the students come to us better prepared in languages. I share the view that we are in danger of becoming a monolingual country in an increasingly interdependent and multilingual world.
                                                      —Henry Rosovsky

---

graduate students who can read anything other than English. Sometimes I wonder whether the foreign language books in our libraries will one day become museum relics. Who will be able to read them? Perhaps the best thing that could happen from the point of view of stimulating foreign language study is for us to fight another war somewhere. That's what produced my own generation of Japanese linguists, Chinese linguists, Russian linguists, and so forth. As soon as the international atmosphere cooled off, both the interest in and incentives for language study declined. Surely there must be a better way to encourage the development of language skills, which are so clearly important in our intellectual and national life. I myself strongly believe in the study of foreign languages as part of a liberal education.

John Ratté: The precedence study which comes to mind in this conversation is the Redbook of the 1940s at Harvard University. A characteristic of that study in general education was that it first examined the situation in the high schools and attempted to make some recommendations which were comprehensive and took as a whole the experience of the student moving through the secondary level and then on into the college. It made recommendations specifically for Harvard which, in turn, were reflected in the curricula of other institutions. I wonder if the dean, or the presidents and the deans, of other institutions, or a person charged with the responsibility

---

Our eleventh- and twelfth-grade students who have been stimulated by the media seem to want many specialized courses. We find it difficult to speak with them about the importance of rigorous college preparation.
—John Ratté

---

for articulation in secondary and tertiary education in any of the states have considered the relationship between the various levels. Have they considered what has been done in the high schools and what should be done in the future? In the last 10 or 15 years the high schools have tended to imitate the colleges. The curricula of my own school and of many other secondary schools are also fragmented. We have a number of electives. Our eleventh- and twelfth-grade students who have been stimulated by the media seem to want a number of specialized courses. We find it very difficult to speak with them about the importance of rigorous preparation for college. Have your Harvard colleagues talked about this in preparing the report?

Henry Rosovsky: In the course of drawing up our curriculum, we thought a great deal about the interrelationship of secondary and tertiary education. Obviously our own thinking had to take account of the kind of preparation we can expect of our students. It might have been an easy way out for us to set very high admissions standards. But the effect of that would be to exclude able and attractive students who may not have had the advantage of first-rate training in secondary school. So we focused our attention on the problem of setting standards for the bachelor's degree, that is, graduation standards.

I agree with Professor Rudolph that questions of primary and secondary education are in many ways more important today than questions of higher education. But I don't think that the colleges can really control what goes on in the high schools. There are many other influences at play on what is, in any event, a highly decentralized educational system. The colleges themselves do not speak with a single voice. Yet the issues ought to concern us all for there is no more central set of institutions in our society than the schools. And they are plainly in a state of disarray, unable to fix priorities among the many—and sometimes conflicting—purposes they are asked to serve.

Robert Marshak: We have been very much concerned about getting back into the high school for a variety of reasons. But before we can deal effectively with the high schools we have to put our own houses in order. For those colleges and universities interested in doing something about the core curriculum, one of the first things that probably ought to be done is to have some serious meetings of liberal arts and science faculty. Frankly, the reason I'm so personally interested in this is that as a scientist I recognize that the emphasis on methodology and concept which we've always given to the students has to be augmented now by the value dimension, the ethical dimension. It's coming up all the time in our society and in the world as a whole. I think the movement should try, somehow, to encapsulate within the core, on the basis of a lot of faculty development and involvement and deliberations, some of the basic knowledge that our young people should have as well as the value questions. When someone talks about alternative curricula, that is fine. No one is saying that this is the only way that the college student is going to receive his education. Besides, the curriculum is only one part of the humane campus environment, which is such an important ingredient in a college education. I personally think that it would be great if some efforts were made in the next couple of years to get people together for lengthy discussions, comparing notes and seeing what can come out of it. Then the next step would be to try to deal with the high schools. To try working with the high schools at this point is premature.

VI

AN ALTERNATIVE: YALE'S DAHL REPORT

In the spring of 1971, Yale President Kingman Brewster appointed a five-member Study Group of Yale College to review Yale's total undergraduate experience. "We badly need a coherent, purposive articulation of the goals of education at Yale," said Brewster, "for those between the high school and postbaccalaureate careers, or graduate and professional training for careers. This will include a rethinking of the objectives and functions of college education." What follow are pertinent excerpts from the Yale study group report, commonly referred to as the Dahl Report after the group's chairman, Robert A. Dahl. The report was never adopted.

What Is Excellence in Undergraduate Education?

At its best, undergraduate education makes special contributions that distinguish it significantly from the formal education that precedes or follows it. But it also shares some qualities of excellence with all good education.

Learning throughout life: Like all education, undergraduate education is excellent to the extent that it nourishes the motivations, arts, and skills needed if one is to continue to develop one's intellectual, aesthetic, and moral capacities throughout the whole span of one's life.

This is hardly a new criterion of excellence. Yet certain features of our present and future world compel us to stress it as a measure of the success or failure of a Yale education in the coming decades. For it is clear that knowledge, information, techniques, and technologies will continue to grow explosively and to change, that an adequate understanding of the world will involve a high and increasing degree of complexity. No matter what one's occupation or life-style may be, informed choices will require continual learning.

In order for learning to continue actively, we believe that one must acquire early and sustain indefinitely a high capacity for acquiring knowledge by independent study, definition of goals, and self-directed search. All higher education should therefore encourage students to ask themselves: What do I want and need to know? How may I best go about learning what I want and need to know? And all higher education should provide students with opportunities to discover answers to these questions in the most effective way. The exploration of these questions ought to be a central, not a marginal, task of a college—perhaps of all education.

If students are to develop and sustain an enduring capacity for acquiring knowledge, we believe that they must be encouraged and allowed to assume as swiftly as they can the principal responsibility for decisions about their own learning. Viewed in this perspective, education ought not to be thought of as a process in which gifted teachers transfer knowledge to resisting students who are cajoled or coerced into acquiring knowledge during certain fixed—and fortunately brief—periods in their lives. Education ought instead to be a process that strengthens a student's own desires for understanding by responding to those desires successfully and in ways rewarding to the student. The pace at which a student can move toward full responsibility for his own education will, of course, vary with student and field. Yet it seems to us absurd to assume that the day he earns his diploma a student will be able to take on the responsibility for his own learning during the rest of his life if he has not already assumed that responsibility during the years before he graduates.

Learning is of many kinds, and we do not deprecate the

value of practical learning. Yet in a world as complex as we know ours to be, one's own direct experience is bound to be an excessively limited, though important, path to knowledge. Even the way one interprets direct experience will depend on categories, assumptions, and ways of thinking brought to that experience and shaped by more indirect ways of encountering knowledge.

On the other hand, except for a minority of our students, lifetime learning will require something other than preparation for the life of the scholar. Most of our students will neither end their formal education on graduating from college nor become PhDs, university teachers, or scholars.

As recently as a quarter century ago, college was pretty much the end of the line in formal education for most Yale students. They assumed that graduating from Yale College provided credentials good enough to insure entry into the careers to which they aspired. This is no longer true. Doubtless it will be increasingly less true over the next 20 years. To more and more students, a college education is regarded as an inadequate preparation for later life. For the majority of our students—and the proportion will probably grow even larger—some sort of further education is felt to be desirable. Like the secondary education of the college-bound student a generation ago, the college years are increasingly followed by some additional period of education—usually of a more specialized kind.

If it is essential to keep this fact before us in considering the future of Yale College, the change must also be kept in accurate perspective. For it is simply not the case, as some of our colleagues may have assumed, that the increasing academic capacity and intellectuality of Yale undergraduates mean that many of them will be scholars. Of the class of 1961, 8 percent earned PhDs; of the class of 1964, 7 percent. Of 970 members of the class of 1964, by 1971 there were 77 teaching, 50 who classified themselves as scientists, and 98 enrolled as students. Thus even by the most generous estimates only a quarter of the members of the class of 1964 were committed to scholarly careers. Subsequent graduating classes have not changed this pattern. In recent years about one senior out of six has planned to begin graduate study in the arts and sciences during the year following graduation. Even counting seniors who said they had plans for eventual graduate study in the arts and sciences, the ratio was less than one in four. Of these, many had in mind careers other than scholarship or teaching. Only around one seventh to one tenth of recent graduates planned careers in education. Around a third had definite plans for law or medical school.

It seems likely, then, that in the near future as in the past only a minority of Yale graduates will go into the world of scholarship, while a majority will probably enter the professions, business, and public affairs. If it is roughly correct to think of undergraduate education as a crucial but not terminal stage in formal education, it is quite wrong to think of it as transitional to a PhD and a life of scholarship, research, and teaching.

Granting that one test of excellence in undergraduate education is the extent to which it strengthens and consolidates predispositions toward continual learning, what is unique or distinctive about the college years? The answer is that for most students these years should provide a special opportunity for establishing certain kinds of intellectual foundations on which later learning may be built. This opportunity is most easily described by two general principles to which Yale College has been committed for half a century: concentration and distribution. The depth of learning achieved in college distinguishes it from secondary school; the breadth of learning distinguishes it from graduate and professional training. The combination lends to undergraduate education its special importance in the development of the students, and, at its best, much of the special intellectual charm of undergraduate education. The scholar-teacher, as we shall argue later, must play a key role at Yale in assuring that students achieve the right combination of distribution and concentration. Yet if the scholar, preoccupied with the complexities of his own subject, forgets that it is undergraduates he teaches, not candidates for the PhD in his field, the principles of distribution and concentration may do little more than expose students to fragments of scholarly learning.

Concentration: By concentrating on a subject, field, discipline, or problem, the undergraduate is expected to acquire more knowledge in depth than he has known heretofore, and thus to gain an understanding of what true mastery might mean. The distinctiveness of the college today is not the mastery of a particular subject or discipline. The average entering freshman at Yale is probably more competent in science and mathematics today than the average graduating senior at Yale a generation ago; few academic subjects can be truly mastered in college—or, for that matter, in a lifetime. Yet the college continues to make an essential contribution. To specialize before college would entail too great a loss of distribution; to seek breadth in graduate and professional education would entail too heavy a cost in acquiring mastery over a field. The college is neither an extension of secondary school nor primarily preparation for graduate and professional training. To be excellent it must be different from both.

What strikes us as wrong with concentration is not the principle but the practice. In many cases, it is appropriate for a student to shape his concentration according to a departmental definition. Yet there are many ways of carving human knowledge, and the departmental slice is only one. If we are to honor the larger principle of concentration we need to free students more than we have in the past from the obligation to major in a departmental field.

Distribution: It is in college that the student first has a chance to acquire enough of a grasp of the major ways of understanding and interpreting the world so that he can begin to make intelligently the choices that will hereafter govern his learning. Secondary education cannot go much beyond equipping a student with the fundamentals; the more specialized education that typically follows college may actually narrow one's range of vision. Undergraduate education should and can fling open the doors.

In view of the need for continual lifetime learning, it would be wrong to think of the principle of distribution as an effort to insure that Yale College graduates are "educated"—as if to *be* educated means to have *been* educated. On the contrary, what distribution should do is provide the best foundation possible for subsequent intellectual, moral, and aesthetic growth.

Problems arise not so much because the principle is wrong but because it is difficult to apply. Few faculty members are prepared to say that students can ignore *their* own particular field. The number of "essential" fields or areas thus threatens to multiply beyond reason. The problem has been attacked by grouping fields into a more manageable number; but any grouping of fields is to some extent arbitrary. Newly emerging areas of knowledge may simply be tucked into conventional categories where they are easily ignored in favor of more traditional subjects.

Finally, the introductory courses to which most students must turn to acquire some understanding of an unfamiliar area are often designed with potential majors in mind and may be poorly suited to the needs of the nonmajor. It is often difficult for highly specialized scholars to take the needs of nonmajors seriously, or to know how to respond to them.

College-as-cafeteria: Faced with difficulties of this kind in applying the principle of distribution, and given the limitations of departments as exclusive bases for concentration, a discouraged faculty could easily give up in despair and simply allow students unrestricted and unguided choices. Yet the college-as-cafeteria easily slides into a disaster of mediocrity. It risks failing in two ways. In the first place, manifold choice is not necessarily sensible choice. The richness and diversity that constitute much of the strength of Yale's educational offerings can be a source of perplexity to the student. The incoming freshman can hardly be expected to grasp more than a fragment of the array before him. Yet even seniors, as they frequently lament, have barely begun to realize, too late, what riches they have passed by. To be sure, some floundering is inevitable and for most students it is, up to a point, probably even desirable. But the fact remains that a multiplicity of choices without adequate information does not make for reasonable choices. To that extent what looks like free choice is in reality often severely limited by ignorance. In these circumstances, a choice that is unintentionally limited by the inexperience of the student is likely to be worse than a choice that is intentionally limited by an experienced faculty.

A second defect of the college-as-cafeteria is the high risk it runs of leaving the student more disoriented than he was when he arrived, without means to gain a sense of direction. Of course students ought to be shaken up by their undergraduate experiences. But to leave them directionless can hardly be one of the desirable aims of education. Typically, during the college years a young person's values begin to crystallize and his perspectives begin to take on coherence; looser, less coherent patterns of development are drawn together to provide ways of interpreting, evaluating, and acting on the world that one carries through life pretty much intact. This integrating process ought not to be indefinitely deferred, and cannot be without great costs to the individual. An uninformed or casually informed search for courses to satisfy largely unexplored purposes seems to us likely to leave the student without much sense of direction in a world where complexity and swift change make it difficult at best to know where one is going.

Responsibilities: To reconcile the faculty's responsibility toward students with the students' responsibility for their own education seems to us to impose certain responsibilities on the college.

First, since not all young people are equally prepared to assume responsibility for their education, Yale has an obligation to admit students who are so prepared. Fortunately, in our judgment, the bulk of the students who now come to Yale are able to take on the kinds of responsibilities we propose. It would be unfair to impose curricular requirements for all simply to control the student who wishes to evade responsibility. Moreover, it would be largely futile, for the one generalization that seems well supported by long experience is that most students who have the will to do so can find a way to beat almost any system of educational requirements. Students who cannot or will not handle the academic responsibilities we propose should not be at Yale.

Second, Yale has an obligation to insure that in assuming responsibilities and making choices, students have appropriate opportunities to be adequately informed. The questions we suggested earlier as central to education—What do I want and need to learn? How may I best go about learning it?—cannot be answered by the student unaided. Students have a right to expect, and the college has an obligation to provide, a satisfactory way of searching for answers. We believe that advice to and consultation with students are presently insufficient at Yale. Nor can we draw much comfort from observing that student advising and consultation seem to be equally or more unsatisfactory at most other institutions of higher education. If the questions we have posed are truly central and not marginal, then the process of student-faculty consultation on programs must move from a marginal to a central position in the activities of both students and faculty members.

Third, however, Yale has an obligation to see that advice and guidance are neither oppressive nor idiosyncratic. If the faculty as a whole has come to believe that it is unwise to impose a single program of instruction on all students, the individual faculty member can hardly be permitted to impose his own particular educational perspectives on the students he is advising. At a minimum, the faculty should continue to express its commitment to the notion that an educated understanding is facilitated by acquiring knowledge of substance or approaches in each of a number of broad divisions of knowledge. Its collective view would serve, as it does now, as a guideline rather than as a set of fixed requirements. In creating a more effective system of advising, the faculty will also need to establish an adequate system of review in order to insure not only that the guidelines have been properly understood and taken into account but also that neither the guidelines, the particular views of an advisor, nor the uninformed choices of a student will impose a program of study poorly suited to the student's educational needs.

Yale's special excellence: We have offered one criterion of excellence that could apply to education in general and two principles that could apply to any liberal arts college. But as we said at the outset, we are dealing with Yale College.

Can Yale make a special, even unique contribution to excellence? We believe so, and a vision of her uniqueness has been central to our conception of Yale College and its educational mission. In an institution of Yale's size, the strength of the college is to be found in a combination of exceptional rarity: The college is small enough to provide much of the accessibility, responsiveness, humaneness, and community that are the virtues of the best independent liberal arts colleges; the university has a scholarly faculty large enough and other resources rich enough to provide undergraduate instruction of extraordinary range and depth.

Yale's opportunity as college and as university is to maximize the benefits of this combination and to minimize its costs. To fulfill this promise seems to us to require at least five conditions:

- Appropriate scale
- Excellence in the faculty
- Excellence in the students
- Excellence in the social, intellectual, and physical setting
- Excellence in the structure and processes of learning and growth.

The Appropriate Range and Limits of Choice

Limits set by faculty resources: Given Yale's commitment to scholarship and the pressing limits on financial resources, it is unlikely that the size or diversity of the faculty can increase measurably over the next decade, or that the number or diversity of the curricular offerings can continue to rise. In fact, it is likely that we have already gone too far on both the graduate and undergraduate levels and must pare down

closer to the core of the curriculum in all fields. This is particularly true if we wish to maintain opportunities for
teaching and learning not only in the context of the large lec-
ture but also in tutorials and small seminars.

Whatever the organization, it is clear that we are facing a
period of strictly limited faculty resources. During the
relatively brief period any given undergraduate is at Yale, he
will necessarily confront a set of courses based in large part
on what the faculty is competent and able to teach. This is
not to say that any student may not learn what he needs to
know in order to pursue his program of study. He must be
given every opportunity to do so individually, for credit, and
with as much assistance and supervision as possible.

It is also clear that over longer periods the faculty can and
should respond to a continuing demonstration of interest in
new areas on the part of the students. However, it is
unrealistic to assume that new courses or programs can be added to the curriculum in the absence of faculty enthusiasm or
expertise and without removing courses or programs that require similar resources.

Options—departmental majors: Departmental majors are
essential for, among other purposes, insuring that Yale College graduates who have successfully completed their majors
will have no difficulty in continuing their education in the
best graduate schools. They are also appropriate for students
who wish to concentrate in areas well represented by departmental activity. In departmental programs, however, it
should be possible to combine some graduate courses with
advanced undergraduate courses, perhaps pairing graduate
and undergraduate students in seminars or tutorials that
could enhance the value of the course for both. While many
such courses might prove to be difficult for all but the
strongest undergraduates, the effort required for a graduate
course is occasionally better invested than in the traditional
senior essay. We recommend therefore that:

> All departmental major programs should be reviewed with an eye
> to providing combinations of graduate and undergraduate
> courses, particularly for students who wish to omit the first year

of graduate or professional training following the Yale College degree. Each department should also consider carefully how its major program can be matched to related graduate or professional programs, so as to permit students to accelerate their total educational program.

Nondepartmental programs of study: The traditional major is still appropriate and generally successful for many Yale undergraduates. Yet only students heading for graduate work in the arts and sciences (less than a quarter)—and not all of them—actually require the departmental major. A growing number of students would prefer, and might obtain greater benefit from, concentration in an area common to a number of disciplines.

What is indeed the justification for the major system in the liberal arts curriculum? It cannot be the need to train every student in depth in some discipline, since relatively few Yale students actually adopt careers in the discipline of their majors. Rather, it arises out of a conviction that one can only understand the significance of the facts, theories, and ideas to which one is exposed in a number of different areas in the course of a liberal arts education if one has penetrated deeply enough into at least one subject to understand the limits on knowledge and the effects that theories and ideas have upon the advancement of knowledge. We share this conviction; but we do not believe that concentration should be limited to subjects in which sufficient work has already been done to lead to the formation of a department. We believe that a substantial fraction of Yale College students of today or of the next decade would be better served by a program of concentration not based on a single department or discipline.

In sum, the college should provide an opportunity for students to concentrate in areas of knowledge or approaches to knowledge not necessarily represented by departments. We therefore recommend that:

> Subject to the guidance and evaluation recommended below, students should have the option of majoring in a department or developing a nondepartmental program of concentration.

The creative arts: The creative arts, by which we mean generally the visual arts, music, and creative writing, should play an active role in the college curriculum as subjects for both distribution and concentration. Indeed, given the importance of these activities in the very definition of a culture, it seems clear that they should be firmly based in the curriculum. By any standard, a liberal education requires familiarity with the history and practice of artistic expression. We therefore believe that substantial activity in one or more of the creative arts should be encouraged in every undergraduate program and that credit should be granted for superior performance.

In attempting to incorporate the creative arts into undergraduate education, a number of institutions have established physical or at least administrative centers for these activities. For a number of reasons we do not recommend moving in this direction at Yale. First, such centers are expensive both in the initial investment required and in their maintenance. While the expense could be justified if it were the only way to achieve the desired result, a single focus for the creative arts is probably not even the best solution. An arts center is likely to be inefficient and redundant because the arts are an integral aspect of other subjects from which they cannot and should not be excised. More important, however, the construction of a center would remove the responsibility for greater concern for the creative arts from the traditional departments, where it should and does rest. It would appear to imply that the creative arts are sharply separate from the accepted intellectual disciplines. It would remove from the arts precisely the critical and analytical approach and scrutiny which they should have. By doing so, it would widen a gap which is already far too wide.

Finally, the construction of a center would tend to lump together aspects of creative work which are in fact quite distinct, and would in all likelihood impose unnecessary restrictions on the development of one or more forms of creative activity. As a university college, Yale is committed to the principle that undergraduate education is best nourished by academic excellence and distinction at the very top of each field. This principle is no less important in the creative arts; it is therefore the professional schools and departments in the creative arts that must supply the strength of undergraduate programs in these areas.

This is not to say that greatly improved physical facilities for the visual arts, for music, and for drama are not needed at Yale. There exists a definite need for substantial new support for studio work, film making, editing and screening, musical performance and practice, and dramatic production. While no new buildings seem to us necessary, additional space will have to be made available, through reorganization and through renovation, in order to meet the needs generated by the increased activity in the creative arts which we are urging.

The major resource which Yale must continue to provide for the creative arts, as for all other activities, is a distinguished and dedicated faculty. A strong program of visiting artists, writers, and performers would be of great value and would take advantage of Yale's location within easy reach of a number of major areas of intense artistic activity. But the success or failure of any program in any one of the arts will depend largely on the faculty at Yale who have chosen to devote a major portion of their energies and talents to teaching as well as to practice. In order to emphasize our commitment to the creative arts in the curriculum and to make possible the kind of development which we look forward to, we have recommended that:

> All faculty members of the university with major responsibilities for the creative arts in Yale College should receive joint appointments to the Yale College faculty.

The existence of a group of teachers and practitioners in the college is essential in order to generate the courses and programs required to implement our guideline and to create the opportunities for independent study in the creative arts which Yale should offer. We believe that coordination with the professional and graduate schools in the creative arts can provide a stronger base for these programs than can the proliferation of additional departments for this purpose. However, resources of the college should be made available to insure that this coordination occurs and that a strong and effective program results. We therefore recommend that:

> The university should attempt to raise the additional funds and to allocate the space needed for the enlarged role of the creative arts in undergraduate education envisioned in this report.

Process of Advice, Guidance, and Evaluation

The structure of requirements, courses, options, terms, and years that helps to define the path of the student through his years in Yale College is an historical product to which thoughtful reflection, conscious intention, the erosions of time, the by-products of past enthusiasms or appointments made for long forgotten purposes, and the sins of omission, inattention, oversight, and plain forgetfulness have all contributed their bit.

Untidiness is not necessarily a vice in education, nor is a well-defined structure—often more illusion than reality— necessarily a virtue.

Nonetheless it seems to us that the structure of Yale College has become too rigid at points where a student's growth requires flexibility and too disorganized where the student would profit from coherence. Thus the difficulty of majoring except in a department is, often, too rigid. Yet a faculty that spends large amounts of time on minor changes in the curriculum has given little attention to the crucial process by which the student learns about courses and majors and decides among the innumerable options.

College mentors—tasks: A pessimist would see Yale as a place where wise and knowing faculty members and intelligent, well-prepared students do not quite meet. There are several fully understandable reasons the encounters are not as frequent or as intellectually moving as they might be, and some of the restraints will persist forever because of the different needs of university scholar and student, older and younger. However, the teaching traditions of Yale College and the potential of the residential college make possible a significant enlargement of the ground where the interests of students and the competence of faculty overlap. We propose, therefore, that a new curricular guidance arrangement be established.

In each of the twelve residential colleges, the dean of Yale College should appoint some fifteen persons—whom we shall call mentors—for terms of approximately three years. This group will be known as the board of mentors of the residential college. Roughly two thirds of the mentors will be faculty members in the university, and one third will be graduate students or members of the university staff. Faculty mentors will be relieved of one half their regular teaching duties. Graduate students who serve as mentors will normally be drawn from those in the later part of their graduate work, and they should be, in pay and perquisites, approximately the equivalent of part-time instructors.

It will be the task of the mentors to advise and guide students in the design of a meaningful course of study, to participate with other mentors in helping students to plan their proposal for the degree, and to take part in the evaluation of the student's accomplishment of his proposal. More concretely, mentors will have four basic responsibilities: advising entering students, helping second year students formulate programs of study, reviewing the plans of third year students, and evaluating the completed work of fourth year students.

First year students—advice on entrance: Each mentor will have primary responsibility for about six to ten entering students, initially assigned to him by the dean on the dean's best guess as to shared interests. Much like the most successful of our present freshman advisors, the mentors will help first year students to plan how they can most meaningfully complete the entering division. Sometimes mentors will know enough about the student and about opportunities at Yale to give advice without calling on colleagues; frequently it will be appropriate for a mentor to seek the counsel of another mentor in his college or another member of the faculty. In any case, mentors will meet as a group, periodically, to review the work of their students, to familiarize themselves with the variety of Yale's offerings, to assess the need for changes in educational opportunities in the college, and to make recommendations to the dean about such changes.

Second year students—planning sessions: The most important responsibility of the mentor is to help the student plan a proposal for the degree. Three mentors from different divisions of the university will form a degree-planning group with their students. Some group meetings may be held in which mentors present statements of their own academic interests and the range of opportunities available in their divisions; other group meetings may be given over to a discussion of the requirements and expectations of graduate and professional schools; smaller groups defined by developing student interests may meet to consider critical questions in their field of interest, procedures that may well involve the preparation of formal essays; and, uniformly, each student will meet with the three mentors, individually and together, to discuss his proposal for the degree and to seek their counsel.

Third year students—review of plans: A student who spends some time away from Yale, particularly one whose leave was planned to play a part in work for the degree, will need to review his proposal and its modification with his mentors on returning to the campus. Less often, a student who does not leave Yale will wish to revise his proposal after an exploratory period implementing it. Finally, a student transferring from outside Yale into the degree division will require review and approval of his proposal in the first weeks of degree division work. The mentor will assist the student in these reviews. It should be noted that a student will not necessarily remain with the same mentor in both entering and degree divisions; however, the mentor involved in review of plans will routinely be concerned as well with the overall evaluation of the student's work.

Fourth year students—evaluation: The process of evaluation, which determines whether a student has satisfactorily completed his program of study and is entitled to the degree, takes place during a student's last semester. It will have several aspects. First, students will meet with the mentors, either individually or in groups, to discuss a program, its strengths and weaknesses, and evidence bearing on the fulfillment of the program. Later, the three mentors themselves will arrive at an evaluation. The nature and extent of their evaluation will necessarily vary with the student and his program. In the case of a departmental major, the three mentors will assure themselves by consulting with the director of undergraduate study that the student has properly fulfilled the requirements of the major. In the case of students with nondepartmental concentrations, the mentors will design and arrange for an appropriate process of evaluation. This will require the mentors to examine grades or other evidence on the quality of the student's work in courses, to consult with other members of the faculty familiar with the student's work, and in some cases to use outside examiners.

Finally, upon approval by the board of mentors in the residential college, the recommendation of the mentors will go to the Yale College Degree Program Committee (described below). It will be the responsibility of the Degree Program Committee to insure that the process of evaluation has been adequate.

Summary of tasks: We have just described the mentorship plan from the perspective of the student moving through the traditional four years. From the perspective of the mentor, tasks appropriate for each group of students will all take place during a given academic year.

> Under the existing calendar, during the first half of the fall semester of any given academic year, the mentor will advise six to ten first year students on their program of studies in the entering division.
>
> During the second half of the fall semester, the mentor will review plans for work in the degree division with his third year students.
>
> Under proposals presented later on, many of these students will be returning from leaves of absence.

During the first half of the spring semester, the mentor and his
second year students will join from time to time with the other
two mentors, and with their students, to discuss their program for
the degree division.

Finally, during the last part of the spring semester the mentors will
determine whether their fourth year students have satisfactorily
completed their program of study.

Although each mentor will be a fellow in a particular
residential college, and his students will ordinarily all be
members of that college, occasionally he may share responsibility for the guidance and evaluation of a few students
from other colleges.

Appointments: Over the years, it is to be hoped that a
large proportion of the Yale College faculty will serve occasionally as mentors. The mentorship must become neither a
permanent duty nor an acquired right. Moreover, the mentors should be drawn from all ranks and divisions of the
university, although some preference should be given to the
appointment of experienced senior faculty. In general, a mentor should be appointed to a term of three years, with no
possibility of reappointment until at least two years have
passed. Furthermore, we recommend that:

The master and dean of each residential college should prepare a
list of nominees for presentation to the dean of Yale College, who,
in consultation with the appropriate departmental chairman or
dean of school, would have final responsibility for the appointment of all mentors.

Governance: We have already mentioned the Degree Program Committee. This committee, appointed by the dean of
Yale College, will have general responsibility for overseeing
the mentorship program. In particular, it will seek to maintain college-wide standards of evaluation; as experience in the
mentorship program accumulates, the committee will formulate methods of evaluation appropriate to particular types
of programs; it will serve as a final court of appeal for a stu-

dent whose proposal is rejected by the board of mentors in his residential college; and it will certify that a student is—or is not—entitled to the degree. We therefore recommend that:

> the dean of Yale College appoint a Degree Program Committee to oversee the function of the mentorship program and to insure that standards appropriate to the college are maintained.

Sequence and Timing of Programs of Study

We propose that the Yale College program be divided into two parts, an entering division and a degree division, which will respectively meet the need for breadth and depth in programs of study.

The purpose of the entering division is to assure that students have some familiarity with the major dimensions of human inquiry and that based on such an acquaintance they can formulate informed plans for degree programs. Students will spend one to two years in the entering division, depending on previous preparation and performance at Yale. Provision will be made to permit students to offer advanced placement credit or equivalency examinations in meeting the entering division requirements. During the period a student is enrolled in the entering division he will normally carry a four course program.

When entering division requirements have been met and a student has prepared an acceptable proposal for a degree, he enters the degree division. Students will be encouraged to take a leave of absence from Yale before they undertake work in the degree division. Students will spend two years in the degree division. Students who elect a standard major must meet departmental requirements for the degree. That portion of the program not set by the department must be approved by the board of mentors. Although there will be no fixed course requirements in the degree division, a student's program will often consist of four courses during each of four semesters. Students who concentrate in an area based on more than one department must have their entire degree program approved by the board of mentors.

The entering division: Despite their high promise and intelligence, students who enter Yale will continue to arrive with widely uneven preparation for independent study. To take account of such variation and to provide new students with a sense of the range of possibilities in the college, the first two to four semesters should normally be spent completing the student's preparation for independent study and helping him explore fields not yet known to him.

The first year special interest seminar: Every new student will join about 15 to 20 of his classmates in a seminar designed to enlarge his understanding of a field of particular interest to him, to assist him in learning the ways of the college, and to give him guided practice in scholarly research and writing. During the summer before first year, the entering student will select, from a list provided him by the college, a special interest seminar which he will attend through the first semester of his stay at Yale. The purposes of the seminars are to deepen the entering student's comprehension of a field of special interest to him and, we hope, to establish a more lasting affiliation, by means of a common intellectual task, with a faculty member and with other first year students. The first year special interest seminars will be led by members of the college faculty and by carefully selected graduate students.

Breadth: While in the entering division, it will be the responsibility of the student and his advisors to warrant that he has some familiarity with the major dimensions of human inquiry and that he is, thereby, ready to enter the degree division. In a university as rich and diverse as Yale, it has long been difficult to specify the fundamental requirements of a liberating education. In Pierson's account of the reforms of 1923, he comments:

> For it is a consequence of the elective system that once the offerings become varied, once the curricular materials are really abundant, it proves next to impossible for a faculty to justify and insist upon any particular combination of courses while barring out others.

Nonetheless, as the college faculty has recognized ever since the introduction of electives, there are broadly defined areas of study which deserve every student's attention. They will vary from time to time according to the strengths of the faculty and the usual preparation of students; they will not always be easily specifiable in terms of traditional disciplinary and departmental divisions; they cannot be uniformly or insensitively required for study; but, withal, the educated free man should, at the very least, have attended to several modes of scholarly search and study. As Yale shifts more toward independent definition of work toward the degree, it is imperative that the entering division assure that the student gains sufficient breadth to make wise use of his independence. Since most entering students have some training in writing English and in the history of the United States, and elect work in those subjects, we are particularly concerned that the entering division provide course work and other ways of understanding abstract and quantitative methods, cultures other than the modern and the Western European, some aspect of artistic expression, the physical world, and biological and social systems. However, we recognize that a sufficient number of appropriate courses do not yet exist to satisfy the range and variety of student interest and preparation in these five areas; therefore, in the long run, it will be necessary for a Committee on Curricular Planning to engage the interest of faculty members in devising profound and appealing ways of studying the areas of breadth. We have a continuing prejudice against the watered and diminished courses for the person who will not be a mathematician or physicist or painter, but while we recognize the peculiar difficulty of inventing courses that maintain their depth and rigor and still meet the student at his level of ability, the need seems to us beyond question. The Dean's Fund should give high priority to the support of ingenious creation of such courses and opportunities.

The exploration of novelty: One of the happiest parts of the first terms of college work is the introduction to areas of study not before known. Yale students have, in the recent past, found new approaches to learning and their lives in disciplines not typically taught in secondary schools, such as philosophy, history of art, and psychology. Mentors should urge the entering student to reach beyond his contemporary understanding and to explore new fields of inquiry. Introductory work in the traditional disciplines may profitably become, over the next years, less "a little bit of everything we know" and more a first statement in depth of the attitudes and methods of the discipline. The aim of the introductory course should not be so much preparation for the discipline as preparation of the student.

Acceleration: Of course, many students will come to Yale already able to meet some of our expectations for the entering division. These students may spend their effort in further study in areas of interest to them or they may propose to their mentors to enter the degree division at the end of two semesters in the entering division. Moreover, intensive summer courses and equivalency examinations should be prepared to permit the dedicated or hurried student to meet the expectations of the entering division outside the usual pattern of study in courses. Acceleration must be approved by the board of mentors and reviewed by the Yale College Degree Program Committee.

The degree division: After having satisfied his mentors as to the adequacy of his preparation for the degree division, a student will, with the advice and counsel of his mentors, prepare a proposal for the degree. The proposal will contain a sensible program of study for the remainder of the student's stay at Yale. The program must be such that its satisfactory completion will warrant the award of the bachelor's degree. No specific number or kinds of courses are required for the proposal. The proposal may consist of a traditional departmental major or a somewhat idiosyncratic arrangement for study; the proposal may represent an integration of college work with continuing education at the level of graduate and professional school; it may, especially for the older student, be defined by specific vocational needs. We anticipate that some students will submit proposals that bridge departments, divisions, even schools, and that others will submit proposals of almost exclusive concentration in a single department. Both kinds of proposals are appropriate, under the guidance of the mentors.

With rare exceptions, a student will spend four semesters in the degree division.

Any faculty member or group of faculty members may design a program representing a cluster of interests or ideas that would be suitable for a proposal for the degree. In addition, the mentors in each college should maintain a notebook of approved proposals that they consider to be especially promising. Sharing of this sort is important for at least two reasons—to widen the student's information about effective proposals and to indicate evolving clusters of shared interests. The degree division program based on individual proposals runs the risk of too much intellectual particularization. However, as intellectually coherent clusters appear in the proposals, arrangements can be instituted to bring closer together students who represent each cluster. Two formal mechanisms can be advanced. First, mentorships in the degree division could be established to represent emerging clusters and mentors could be chosen in the light of the emerging definition of shared interests. Second, new courses on the administrative model of the residential college seminars could be invented as intellectual meeting places for students in each cluster. Like all new courses, these would be shown to the Course of Study Committee for approval.

The usual process of review and approval of a proposal for the degree would take the following course. During the planning sessions, a student will seek out the advice and recommendations of his mentors. When the mentors are satisfied with his proposal, they will forward it to the board of mentors of his college (the group of 15 who serve as mentors for each residential college). Under most circumstances, the board of mentors will have the final decision about whether or not the proposal is sound. If, however, the board of mentors does not approve the proposal, the student may submit the proposal to the Degree Program Committee. That committee will also review all cases in which a student's work is judged inadequate by the mentors after their evaluations.

Summary recommendation on mentorships: In the light of the foregoing discussion, we recommend that:

Yale College should develop a degree sequence based on an entering division and a degree division. The general supervision of the student's work in these divisions should be entrusted to college mentors. These mentors, of whom there should be about 15 in each residential college, will be appointed by the dean of Yale College in consultation with the relevant residential college master and department chairman or school dean. The mentors will advise students as they enter Yale, help them plan their proposal for the degree, and evaluate their overall performance. These programs, and the mentors' evaluation of them, will be subject to review by the Degree Program Committee. Each student will spend two years in the degree division. The number of courses he takes in that division will vary with the program. Depending on the student's ability to meet the guidelines and prepare a satisfactory proposal for the degree, the student will spend two to four semesters in the entering division. In the entering division, the student will normally take four courses each semester.